Creative Grammar Practice

Getting

learners

to use both

sides of

the brain

Pilgrims

LONGMAN

**Günter Gerngross
and Herbert Puchta**

Pearson Education Limited
Edinburgh Gate, Harlow
Essex CM20 2JE, England
and Associated Companies throughout the world.

© Longman Group UK Limited 1992

This book is produced in association with Pilgrims
Language Courses Limited of Canterbury, England.

First published 1992
Seventh impression 1999

Set in 10/12 ITC Cheltenham Book
Printed in Malaysia, TCP

British Library Cataloguing in Publication Data
Puchta, Herbert
Creative Grammar Practice: Getting Learners to Use Both
Sides of the Brain.
– (Pilgrims Longman Resource Books Series)
I. Title   II. Gerngross, Gunter   III. Series
425

ISBN 0 582 08957 3

Acknowledgements
We are grateful to the following for permission to reproduce
copyright material:
HarperCollins Publishers, Inc for an extract from *Tao Te Ching*
by Stephen Mitchell (Harper & Row, 1988), copyright © 1988
by Stephen Mitchell; Prentice Hall, a division of Simon &
Schuster, Inc, for an extract by *Ann Landers Says . . . Truth
is Stranger* by Ann Landers (Revised Edition, 1968), © 1968;
the author's agent for the poem 'Mart's Advice' from *You
Tell Me* by Michael Rosen (Viking Kestrel); Scholastic
Publications Ltd for the poem 'From A Problem Page' from
Wouldn't You Like To Know by Michael Rosen (Puffin Books,
1980).
We have been unable to trace the copyright holder in two
poems by Karla Kuskin from *Dogs and Dragons, Trees and
Dreams* (Harper & Row, First Edition, 1980).

We are grateful to the following for their permission to
reproduce copyright photographs:
Reflections Photolibrary for page 117.

Illustrations
Cover illustrated by Michaela Blunden
Illustrations by Kathy Baxendale and John Farman

A letter from the Series Editors

Dear Teacher,

This series of teachers' resource books has developed from Pilgrims' involvement in running courses for learners of English and for teachers and teacher trainers.

Our aim is to pass on ideas, techniques and practical activities which we know work in the classroom. Our authors, both Pilgrims teachers and like-minded colleagues in other organisations, present accounts of innovative procedures which will broaden the range of options available to teachers working within communicative and humanistic approaches.

We would be very interested to receive your impressions of the series. If you notice any omissions that we ought to rectify in future editions, or if you think of any interesting variations, please let us know. We will be glad to acknowledge all contributions that we are able to use.

Seth Lindstromberg
Series Editor

Mario Rinvolucri
Series Consultant

Pilgrims Language Courses
Canterbury
Kent
CT1 3HG
England

Günter Gerngross

Herbert Puchta

Günter Gerngross is a professor of English at the Pädagogische Akademie in Graz, Austria and teaches EFL at Graz University. He has a PhD in education and is still very much engaged in classroom practice. He has been teaching children, teenagers and adults for more than 20 years. He is also involved in teacher training in Austria and has run teacher training seminars in Slovenia and Hungary. He has written a number of coursebooks, research papers and articles, mostly in collaboration with Herbert.

Herbert Puchta is a professor of English at the Pädagogische Akademie in Graz, Austria. He has a PhD in language teaching pedagogy. Among his publications are a number of coursebooks and resource books for teachers. He regularly works for Pilgrims and has done workshops in France, England, Spain and Greece. He has also worked for the British Council. Herbert has a professional interest in psychology and is a master practitioner of NLP (Neuro Linguistic Programming).

Günter and Herbert are presently working on a book on how to use creative visualisation in EFL classes. They are experimenting with new ways to foster learners' self-esteem and build trust in the classroom while, at the same time, maintaining an effective programme of accuracy-oriented language learning.

Contents

Index of lessons

Acknowledgements

Thanks to:

- our families for being what they are and for their continuous support.
- Hans-Eberhard Piepho for various discussions during a grammar workshop in Rauischholzhausen, in his car, on walks, and over cheese and wine. In these talks the spark of *Creative Grammar Practice* began to glimmer. We should like to add that this was not the only spark that originated from contacts with Hans-Eberhard.
- Mario Rinvolucri for his comments at an early stage of the manuscript and for being a friend and mentor for many years whose ideas have frequently brought new perspectives and insights into our work.
- Earl W. Stevick, whose books have had a lot of influence on our work.
- Robert Dilts for what he taught us about creativity and the mental strategies of outstanding people. (See bibliography for details of published work.)
- the many teachers who readily allowed us to try out our ideas in their classrooms and who supported us with their comments and enthusiasm. Also their students for their energy and creativity and for providing a number of texts in this book.
- the teachers from the Landesarbeitsgemeinschaft Steiermark and Niederösterreich. Cooperating with them over the years has been a supportive and challenging experience.
- colleagues at two British Council Specialist Workshops in Canterbury 1990, at two Acrea-Pilgrims-IATEFL conferences in Paris 1989 and 1990, the International Conference for Teaching Foreign Languages in Barcelona, the GRETA Conference in Granada and the British Council Conference in Vienna (all in 1991) for their valuable comments and for some of the texts in this book.
- a number of colleagues for their support and comments: Tessa Woodward, John Morgan, Rick Cooper, Adrian Underhill, Nathalie Hess, Robin Davis, Judy Baker and all those at the Pilgrims Technical Evenings in summer 1990.
- Peter Worley of Hilderstone College for allowing us to write what he called our 'memoirs' up in room 8 under the roof.
- Rosie Tanner for her exhilarating support.
- Edith Rainer for her word processing skills and for her support and enthusiasm.

A special thank you to Seth Lindstromberg for combining human qualities with being the most professional editor one can imagine.

Günter Gerngross   Herbert Puchta
Graz   Trofaiach
1992   1992

Introduction

OVERVIEW

This is a practical book. It offers teachers a variety of lessons and activities for everyday use in their foreign language classes. The ideas presented here have worked in a variety of teaching situations. We have taught all the lessons ourselves and have benefited from feedback from students and from colleagues. We believe that what has been enjoyable and successful in our classes will bring similar results in other teaching situations with younger learners as well as with adults.

We have not attempted to cover all possible grammar points. The language structures we focus on in this collection are ones which our research into classroom practice and feedback from teachers of various nationalities have shown to be particularly difficult to get across successfully. We have also tried to include a wide range of techniques which teachers can draw on when teaching grammar points not covered here.

The 53 grammar lessons that form the core of the book are for practising grammar points that have already been presented. That is, our basic assumptions for each grammar structure are that its meaning/use/function has already been taught more or less successfully and that what your students need now is guided practice. For the basic purpose of affording practice, each lesson is complete. There are suggestions for warming up and leading into the lessons as well as ideas for rounding them off. For purposes other than provision of guided practice, each lesson is variously adaptable. One adaptation, for example, is to use the model text in initial presentation in order to clarify use, form and function of the grammatical concept to be introduced.

We hope that both you and your students will find that grammar practice does not have to be the all too typical dull routine. Our aim is to stimulate the imagination, humour and creativity of your learners. We think that once you become familiar with the ideas behind these lessons, you will find it natural to adapt them to your and your learners' needs and will discover that grammar practice can be fun.

LEARNING GRAMMAR THROUGH RULES

Many adult learners have a very strong need to understand the rules according to which grammatical structures are formed. They also frequently insist on being given rules about how and when a certain bit of language is used. For these learners, teaching with reference to explicit rules has definite advantages. There is practically no evidence,however, that the same is true for all adult learners, or for children and teenagers. Young learners especially (and some adults too) seem to be more at ease with holistic methods of learning grammar in which structures are acquired subconsciously. Additionally, there are mountains of evidence that many learners, of whatever age or tendency in learning style, are unable to transfer good formal knowledge of grammar to effective use. Such discrepancy between knowledge and putting it to use has led us to look for alternative ways of helping teachers to manage the practice of grammar in a more efficient way.

Earl Stevick's research has encouraged us in our search. In Stevick (1989) he analyses the widely varying strategies used by seven excellent language learners. One of these, Ed, is a highly successful learner who draws on three resources when speaking or writing:

● explicit rules
● remembered sentences and sentence fragments
● feelings derived from 'experiences with how a change at one point in a sentence will require a change somewhere else', that is, instincts about regularities or patterns.

Stevick concludes: 'All these kinds of resources are linked to one another, and so they help to retain one another in Ed's memory. The good thing about regularities and remembered fragments is that they operate more quickly than rules.' (p. 94.)

Henry Widdowson has summed up additional evidence from recent studies:

Traditionally, second language pedagogy has assumed that the main difficulty for the learner lies in the acquisition of syntax. Learn the sentence patterns and then slot the words in. But so many words just do not fit. Learn the rules and then apply them. But the problem is to know when and where they apply. There are bound to be some exceptions. But there seem to be so many. Indeed the whole language seems to consist not so much of well-regulated generative mechanisms as lexical chunks of varying size and variable syntactic adaptability.
(From a talk at the ELT Conference in Vienna in 1989.)

There is hence a significant body of opinion that for some learners what is needed is the learning and recollection of bits of text exemplifying useful 'sentence patterns' and word or phrase use. Our experience is that such learners are in the majority, certainly among the young. Our book is designed to help you teach grammar to this common kind of learner.

LEARNING GRAMMAR AND THE HUMAN BRAIN

One model of the location of different thinking styles and skills in the brain holds that our left brain hemisphere is 'the analyst' within us while the right hemisphere is 'the poet'. Another model has it that any given brain cell, in either hemisphere, can fulfil both 'analytic' and 'poetic' functions. Whichever is the case, it is important to recognise that many learners have a broad tendency in learning style towards the one or the other, with younger learners especially being more 'poetic'. Grammar, to the extent that it involves analysis, is a (so-called) left hemispheric domain and thus extremely difficult for 'poetic' learners to succeed in. We hope to show, however, how to do solid, effective grammar work in a non-analytic fashion.

In his book *Righting the Educational Conveyor Belt* (1989), Michael Grinder reviews the ties between age, brain hemispheres and preferences in learning styles. He concludes that some people process, store and recall information more easily if it is presented visually while others prefer auditory or kinesthetic (movement and touch) modes. The clear message here is that teachers need to know how to balance their reliance on visual, auditory and kinesthetic input modes if they are to cater successfully for individual learning styles within a group. One of our major concerns has been to show ways of providing such balance.

GRAMMAR MEMORY AND THE IMPACT OF THE CONTENT

Stevick (1976, p.44) suggests that content and emotional depth of experience are also crucial factors in the acquisition of grammar. In other words, when it comes to teaching the genitive -s, a sentence like Martin Luther King's 'I want to be the white man's brother not his brother-in-law' will be better and longer remembered than 'The man's hat is green'. Accordingly we have tried to incorporate into our model texts as much wit, metaphor, humour, fancy, absurdity and other imaginative devices as possible. The aim in doing this is to make these texts, and the language in them, as memorable as possible. Additionally – we believe – if the model texts are memorable, the corresponding student texts and the target language they include are more likely to be memorable too. Without memory, of course, there can be no learning. Accordingly, besides trying to provide examples of memorable content, we have attempted to include as many memory enhancing activities of all kinds as we could. (See, for example, 'Anchoring' on p. 8.)

FINDING YOUR LESSON

Suppose you need a lesson to practise *if*-sentences. How do you proceed? First, look in the index under *if*. You will see that there are four lessons to choose from (lessons 4.1, 4.3, 4.5 and 4.10). One by one, look these lessons up and decide which is best for your class. Then read the one you have chosen more carefully to see whether you need to adapt it in any way. Often, our lesson recipes include alternatives at various stages. However, there is another source of ideas for adapting a lesson at a given stage. For example, if you feel you need a different technique or task-type at the 'Text creation' stage, look at the 'Text creation' stages in a few other recipes – even ones on quite different teaching points. You are bound to come across a range of different ways of proceeding. Finally, the 'General techniques' section offers a range of general options applicable to every lesson and it may well include something to help you adapt a lesson you have chosen.

THE STAGES OF THE LESSONS

Most of the lessons follow the same sequence of stages: lead-in, presentation of the model text, reconstruction of the model text, text creation and text sharing. We do not mean to suggest that this sequence should never be varied. However, general adherence to this sequence has the following advantages: a gradual lead-in to a lesson opens up a field of awareness; the model text, if conspicuously presented, affords intensive input of the target structure(s); reconstruction of the model text provides ample opportunity for guided practice; the writing phase (text creation) gives students a highly motivating opportunity to express themselves creatively and - given the previous phases of the lesson - accurately; the sharing of texts which follows injects the stimulating spark of student-to-student communication.

Lead-in activities

These are for:
- generally warming everyone up and getting them ready to work in a foreign language;
- developing awareness of and interest in the topic you're going to work with;
- bringing known words back to mind and teaching new ones.

A basic lead-in activity is the brainstorm. A few of our lessons don't come with lead-ins of their own. For these, a brainstorm is a good way to start (see Hess 1991, p.XIV for different ways of organising brainstorms). Or borrow a lead-in from other lessons here.

Presentation of model text

A model text is a short text which not only shows the written form of the target structure, but clarifies its meaning/use/function. Presentation of the text (not to be confused with presentation of a given target structure in a text) is the process of familiarising the students with the model text. This can be done in various ways. You can dictate the text or they can read it on OHP or on a handout. Often, however, presentation phases involve the students more actively in the construction of the model text, e.g. you begin with a gapped version and elicit the missing words from them.

Reconstruction of model text

Reconstruction of a model text can be done in spoken or written form. It is the process of eliciting from the students as accurately as possible the text presented to them earlier. The rationale of this stage is this: by remembering the model text the students can experience a feeling of success and gain ability in using the structure(s) accurately. In using different lessons from *Creative Grammar Practice* you will encounter various ways of organising text reconstruction, such as use of gesture, pictures and written prompts.

Text creation

This is where your students create their own text within the framework of the model they have been working with. Naturally, your students will often want to know new vocabulary. Supply the words they ask for or make sure they have access to a bilingual dictionary. We have favoured writing for this phase as experience has shown that students find it far easier to be creative in writing. Writing also allows greater focus on accuracy since students have the time to reflect, correct, discard and add. It allows text creation in pairs or small groups and can therefore generate much task-focused speaking. Finally, the products can be displayed and/or used in other ways.

If, however, you want your students to create their texts orally, we suggest the following procedure:
1 Form pairs or small groups.
2 Provide each group or pair with a cassette recorder.
3 Ask them to create a text orally. One of them says the text out loud and this text is recorded.
4 The students listen to the recording of the text. If they spot any errors, they make a new recording.
5 You listen to the cassette and comment on language correctness.
6 Students make a new recording incorporating your suggestions.
7 All the pairs or groups present their recordings to the class.
All this would hardly be possible in normal, unrecorded oral production.

BASIC TECHNIQUES

We have found the following techniques helpful in transferring the grammar structures (in the form of sentence fragments) into students' long term memory.

Silent time

H A Klauser (1986, p. 90) suggests allowing a period of silence before any creative writing. She claims that this 'daydreaming' or 'drifting off' is of great importance for getting ready to write. We are not suggesting here, that a silent time before the creative writing is an absolute must. However, our students have always commented favourably on such a silent phase. It seems that the silent time helps the students get into contact with their 'poetic selves' and thus access their creativity. (We sometimes use meditative music to accompany the silent time.)

Reading out loud by the teacher

In several lessons we suggest that you read out the model text after the learners have reconstructed it. Preferably, they should have their eyes closed. This 'straight-through' clear hearing of the text helps students to create a holistic image of it. The reading also provides a model of pronunciation and intonation; one that seems especially effective if students are reflectively listening with eyes closed. Finally, this reading can be essential as a means of 'anchoring' the structure and elements of the text in the minds of those students whose main channel of intake is auditory.

Managing students' reading out loud

Our experience is that students profit greatly from reading out loud themselves if and only if they have adequate rehearsal. The best known form of rehearsal is in teacher-led, whole class repetition of difficult bits. But, if you are asking students to read out their own texts, more student-centred rehearsal is appropriate. Before asking students to read out loud, tell them to:
1 Read through their texts silently looking for words they aren't sure how to pronounce. They can then ask or check in a dictionary.
2 Rehearse by reading the text sub-vocally, that is by silently moving lips, tongue and other vocal 'apparatus'.
3 Practise making pauses so the audience can follow them well and using the pauses to have eye contact with their audience.
Ask them to read out loud, clearly and slowly. Remind them that the audience suffers if a speaker's subconscious attitude while reading out loud is 'I want to get this over with as quickly as possible'.

Correction as editing

Errors are unavoidable when learners write texts. You need to understand this and treat learners' texts sympathetically. However, we have noticed that learners typically have a strong desire to improve the accuracy of their texts if they know that these will be shared later on (see 'Publication of the learners' texts' below). This follow-on accuracy work, or *editing*, is the process whereby the students themselves, other students, and/or you read their written work and suggest changes which can be incorporated in a new version of that work.

Editing takes place either while students are writing (you walk round and suggest changes) or after the students have finished. Editing is important since it increases learner awareness of appropriate forms. Also, for our method, learner texts need to be accurate since they serve as additional input in various follow-on activities (see 'Publication of learners' texts' and 'Anchoring' below).

It is important to let your students know that their texts will not be corrected as if they were tests. Your students should come to regard any correction as a means whereby they can better edit their work before sharing or 'publication'. Your attitude is decisive here: rather than tally errors, do everything necessary to help the learners with the process of finalising and improving their products. You can best do this by never using discouraging language. Klauser (1986, p.89) recommends language such as 'I think you need ...', 'Maybe you could note ...', etc. The main options in the editing of student texts are:

The teacher as editor
After finishing their texts, students hand them in and you correct all the errors. This can be done in class – while other students are still writing – or after the lesson.

The teacher as a gentle editor
You correct only what you think your students cannot correct themselves. Underline auto-correctable errors (those you assume the students are able to correct themselves) in pencil. The students then go through their texts a second time trying to correct what you have underlined, possibly also consulting classmates, using a dictionary and/or checking with the model text(s). In an informal study we carried out with teenagers in their fourth year of English sixty percent of all the errors were successfully corrected using this editing mode.

Other learners as editors
When students have finished writing, ask them to work in pairs and to exchange their texts. Get them to help each other by suggesting changes on the texts before these are handed in to you.

Publication of the learners' texts

We have found each of the following methods successful:

a Regularly use a text-board to display (neat) copies of student texts, preferably together with other visuals selected by you and your students. Your text-board can be a cork-board set aside for this purpose or poster paper stuck on the walls of the classroom.

b Get students to read out their texts to the class. Involve them in giving feedback, for example saying what they like about others' texts. This can contribute greatly to a readiness on the students' part to listen to each other and treat each other with more respect.

c Suggest that students collect their texts in a special individual or class journal. Getting your students to read their journal(s) from time to time can contribute enormously to their own assessment of their progress over a period of time.

Anchoring

The following techniques for helping students remember grammar points have proved helpful in our trial classes. You can teach some of them to your students so that they can use them on their own at home (or in class). Others are mainly for classroom use. After trying out some of these techniques, you might like to discuss their usefulness with your students in order to find out what works best.

Learners anchor their own texts
After the final editing ask your students to memorise their own texts. This can be done in various ways:

a Read the first line of the text out loud. Once able to remember it, they add the second line and so on.

b Read the full text as often as necessary in order to be able to recite it completely. This may be accompanied by inner voicing or muttering, a technique especially effective for learners who are very auditory in their learning style.

c Read through the text. Students try, while doing so, to form a striking mental image for each line, one that will help them to remember the line. Mental images can be visual representations of what has been read, or sounds, feelings, smells, or tastes or any combination of these. Closing the eyes can facilitate this mental imagery. (For example, see 1.6.)

d Walk up and down saying the text to themselves line for line.

e Write the text or parts of the text (especially the ones which are difficult to remember) in the air. They close their eyes and imagine seeing the text in the air or on an imaginary board or TV screen.

f Record the text on a cassette recorder and learn it by listening to it several times.

g Underline various parts of the text in different colours, draw on it or scribble down anything that will help them recall the text. If you are leading this work, give students some time to study the text. Then you/they remove it and they write it down from memory (in class or at home). Give them time to check their version with the original.

h Work in pairs. Each learner produces a gapped version of their own texts. Their partner should fill in the appropriate words in each gap. Depending on the level of the class, the words that have been omitted can be given in a box underneath the text. Alternatively, only the first letter of each missing word can be given.

i Get students to work in pairs, each student dictating their own text to their partner. Each learner then corrects their partner's text.

Learners anchor someone else's text

After the final editing, display all the texts that your learners have written on the walls of the classroom. Ask everyone to stand up and choose one text that they would like to memorise (not their own).

Get them to copy this text into their own note book – without taking it off the wall. Students try to remember as much of these texts as they can, then go back to their desks and note down what they can remember. Then they go back to the texts again and so on.

Encourage your students to memorise the texts they have copied. Then collect all the texts from the wall and either ask for recitations of individual texts ('Who can quote José's text?') or read out some words from a text. See if anyone can recite the whole text or follow on from the bit you've started with.

Learners anchor other texts

After the final editing ask your learners to memorise as many texts as they can within a given time (e.g. five minutes). Then arrange students in groups and get them to find out who can remember the most texts within each group.

Learners anchor parts of texts

a Underline various parts of each text with different coloured pencils and display the texts on the walls of the classroom. (For example, underline individual words that you would like your class to remember in green, certain structures in red, other structures in blue). Ask your learners to walk round and remember the underlined parts of the texts. Then call out one of the colours. The learners quote as many of the words and structures they can remember that were underlined in that colour.

b Use a tambourine to beat the rhythm of one of the underlined sentences. The learners guess the sentence. (Thanks to Glen Stephen for this idea.)

c Another technique involves all students in reading several texts each and remembering sentences from them which they especially like. Give students time to memorise a set of favourite sentences in different texts. Ask them to quote the sentences they like without looking at the texts. This technique is especially effective in revision following a sequence of grammar exercises. (This technique is based on Stevick's drilling model, 1976, p.76.)

CHAPTER 1

Basic phrase patterns

1.1

GRAMMAR
Language of
description

LEVEL
Lower
intermediate +

TIME
40–60 minutes

EXTRAS
(Optional) class
set of handouts of
yes/no questions;
class set of
handouts of
skeleton text

WRITE ABOUT A BAG

Lead-in activities

Guessing objects

1 Ask everyone in class to think of an object.
2 After a while, choose a student and start asking *yes/no* questions in order to find out what object they have in mind. For example:

Is it in this room?
Is it made of …?
Is it expensive/cheap/red/ …?
Is it longer/smaller than a …?
Is it as big/expensive/ … as …?
Can you …?
Have you got one?
Do you need it every day?

Repeat with several students so that your class get an opportunity to hear a range of questions several times. To give your students further practice in asking questions, pair them up and let them repeat this guessing game over the course of a few lessons.

VARIATION

1 Ask your students to split up into three or four groups and to sit or stand in different corners of the room.
2 Ask one member of each group to come to you. Show them a word for an object, e.g. *umbrella*.
3 The 'messengers' go back to their groups. The members of each group have to ask their 'messenger' questions to find out what the object is. The 'messengers' are, of course, not allowed to give any help by mime or gesture, etc. When a group has guessed the object they send another 'messenger' to you to be shown the next word. The group that guesses three words in a row first wins.

An object that means something to me

1 Talk briefly about an object that means something to you. For example:

I've had this bag for years. I got it from a friend who bought it in India and gave it to me as a present. Its colours are not bright any more but I still like it. It smells nice and I sometimes think of India when I look at it.

2 Ask the students to close their eyes and visualise an object that is special to them. Allow two or three minutes for this.

3 Tell them to get into groups of three and to talk about their object.

Listen and guess

1 Read out text A twice. (Don't fill in the blank.) Before the second reading ask your students to close their eyes and imagine the object as vividly as possible.

Text A

Too many people write about love.
I want to write about my _____.
It's brown and smooth,
a present from Dad.
I've had it since I was nine
and I've always found it again
when I've lost it.
I sometimes smell it
when I put it on
and it always reminds me
of saddles and horses.

2 Ask your students to say what they think the object is. (It's a belt.)

Presentation of model texts

1 Present texts B and C on the board or provide photocopies.

2 Ask the students to fill in the blanks for both texts.

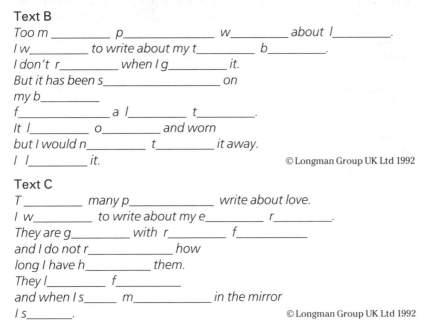

Text B

Too m _____ p_____ w_____ about l_____.
I w_____ to write about my t_____ b_____.
I don't r_____ when I g_____ it.
But it has been s_____ on
my b_____
f_____ a l_____ t_____.
It l_____ o_____ and worn
but I would n_____ t_____ it away.
I l_____ it.   © Longman Group UK Ltd 1992

Text C

T _____ many p_____ write about love.
I w_____ to write about my e_____ r_____.
They are g_____ with r_____ f_____
and I do not r_____ how
long I have h_____ them.
They l_____ f_____
and when I s_____ m_____ in the mirror
I s_____.   © Longman Group UK Ltd 1992

3 Read out the original texts (see keys below). Get your students to listen and check what they have filled in.

Text B (key)
Too many people write about love.
I want to write about my teddy bear.
I don't remember when I got it.
But it has been sitting on
my bookshelf
for a long time.
It looks old and worn
but I would never throw it away.
I love it.

Text C (key)
Too many people write about love
I want to write about my earrings.
They are green with red flowers
and I do not remember how
long I have had them
They look funny
and when I see myself in the mirror
I smile.

Text creation

1 Write the following prompts on the board. Ask your students to write their own text based on these prompts.

Too many people write about love.
I want to_____
I _____ (since/for _____)
_____
It's _____

2 After editing (see page 7) get some students to read out their texts to the class.

Here are two texts, the one on the left written by a thirteen-year-old, the one on the right by Janice Tabe at a teacher training workshop.

Too many people write about love.
I want to write about my skateboard.
It's a present from my parents and I
like it very much.
It was very expensive and the deck
alone cost a fortune.
It's black and green and looks
fantastic
It's the best present I've ever had.

Too many people write about love.
I want to write about my big feet.
I don't remember when I got them
but they've been at the end of
my legs for a long time
They look old and worn but
I would never cut them off.
I need them.

FEAR IS THE COLOUR OF A GREY, POLLUTED RIVER

Lead-in activities

Story telling

1 Write the following words on the board. Explain any your students are not familiar with:

*love   hatred   fear   boredom   anger
disappointment   happiness   sadness   joy*

2 Talk about two or three incidents from your life exemplifying the emotions above, for example:

I once spent a night alone on a lonely beach. When it was dark, I could suddenly hear all kinds of unfamiliar sounds and noises. I began to be afraid there might be snakes, spiders and scorpions. And then I was seized with the fear that somebody might come along and kill me. I finally fell asleep but I had bad dreams.

Another incident I remember is once coming upon a group of boys who were holding an animal down. When they noticed me they let go of it and I saw that they had tied a big plastic toy to a cat's tail. The cat ran off miaowing. I ran after it, caught it, and, after a struggle, managed to cut the string with my pocket knife. I was very angry with those boys, but they ran away while I was trying to help the animal.

3 Ask your students to work in groups of three or four. Tell them to pick one word from the box and to make notes about an incident or situation that goes with their word.
4 In their groups they then take turns reading out their notes. (They don't need to make sentences.) The other group members try to guess what emotion the incident/situation was all about. The author confirms or denies the guesses and elaborates as requested.

Presentation of model text

Show your students the gapped text on the OHP (or write it on the board) and ask them to guess the missing words. Whenever someone has guessed a word correctly, fill it in.

Gapped text
Happiness _____ the colour of poppies in spring.
It _____ like chocolate ice cream.
It _____ like peach blossom.
It _____ like the cry of the eagle
and it _____ like the wide open sky.

GRAMMAR
Something is the colour of/ something smells, sounds, tastes like

LEVEL
Lower intermediate +

TIME
50 minutes

EXTRAS
(Optional) OHP transparency with model text

Model text
Happiness is the colour of poppies in spring.
It tastes like chocolate ice cream.
It smells like peach blossom.
It sounds like the cry of the eagle
and it looks like the wide open sky.

Text creation

1 Write a list of feelings on the board. Ask your students to choose one feeling from the list. Everyone writes their own text based on the structure of the model text. If you want to give your students some more examples before they start writing, there are three texts below which were written by thirteen-year-old learners in their third year of English.
2 When finished, students read their texts out loud or display them in the classroom.

Example texts
Happiness *is the colour of red flowers.*
It smells like the flowers in a small garden.
Happiness sounds like the singing of a hippo in the water.
Happiness makes me dance rock and roll.

Hatred *is the colour of black and red devils.*
It tastes like a bitter lemon,
it smells like death
and it looks like the darkest night.
Hatred sounds like thunder.
It makes me feel depressed.

Fear *is the colour of a grey, polluted river.*
It smells like the fumes of factories
and it looks like a ghost.
It sounds like the howling of wolves.
Fear makes me think of problems.

FLOWERS, TIGERS, MOUNTAINS AND TALL TREES

Preparation

For Step 2 of the variation on page 17 make strips of paper with words/word groups on them.

Lead-in activities

Make your choice
1 Hand out photocopies of worksheet A below. If photocopying is not possible, write the texts and the missing words on the board or on an OHP.
2 Tell the students to fill in the blanks with words from the box to create two meaningful texts. Make sure everyone understands the last two lines of each text.

WORKSHEET A

There are _____   *There are* _____
there are _____   *there are* _____
there are _____   *there are* _____
there are _____   *there are* _____
and _____   *and* _____
when I take a long look   *when I look out of my*
into your eyes.   *little tent in the dunes.*

> *kites of every colour – high mountains*
> *– flowers – tigers – white clouds –*
> *fireworks over dark lakes – tall trees*
> *– high waves – seagulls crying –*
> *surfboards jumping*

© Longman Group UK Ltd 1992

3 Get several students to read out their texts.
4 Ask your students which of the class's texts they like best.
5 Then read out the texts below.

WORKSHEET A (KEY)

There are flowers   *There are white clouds*
there are tigers   *there are seagulls crying*
there are tall trees   *there are high waves*
there are high mountains   *there are surfboards jumping*
and fireworks over dark lakes *and kites in all colours*
when I take a long look   *when I look out of my*
into your eyes.   *little tent in the dunes.*

1.3

GRAMMAR
There is/there are

LEVEL
Elementary +

TIME
50 minutes

EXTRAS
(Optional) class set of handouts of worksheets A and B; ten paper strips (40 x 15cm each); Blu-Tack

Text creation

The students write their own texts using the gapped texts in worksheet A as models. They read out their texts or display them.

VARIATIONS

a You may choose to offer only the following prompts:

There are _____
there are _____
there are _____
there are _____
and _____
when _____
_____ .

b You may offer them additional text endings, such as:

in the picture I'm going to paint
when I'm daydreaming in the classroom
when I'm looking down from my hang glider
when I remember . . .
in the film I'd like to make
when I think of . . .

Presentation of more model texts

1 Hand out copies of worksheet B or write the texts on the board and proceed in the same way as Steps 1 – 5 above.

WORKSHEET B

There is _____   *There is* _____
there is _____   *there is* _____
there is _____   *there is* _____
there is _____   *and* _____
and _____   *in the town I hate living in.*
in the film I'd like to make.

> *a gangster – too little sun – no park*
> *– a sheriff – a carriage – a small*
> *town – lots of gold – a lot of traffic*
> *– too much noise*

2 When the students have read out their texts, present the key:

WORKSHEET B (KEY)

There is a small town   *There is a lot of traffic*
there is a sheriff   *there is too much noise*
there is a gangster   *there is too little sun*

there is a carriage   *and no park*
and lots of gold   *in the town I hate living in.*
in the film I'd like to make.

Text creation

1 Again, you have a choice of prompts. Depending on the level and creativity of your group, you can include the last sentence in the model. One student who was offered all the prompts, including the last sentence, wrote this:

There is a swimming pool
there is a cinema
there is a park
there is a nice school
and lots of sun
in the town I love living in.

2 Encourage everyone to write texts using both *there are* and *there is* in their texts. Get students to also include quantifiers such as *lots of, hardly any, few*, etc.

Here is a text written by a twelve-year-old. In her class we had presented model texts featuring *There are ...* and *There aren't any ....*

There aren't any gangsters
there aren't any monsters
there aren't any policemen
there aren't any accidents
in the film I'd like to make.

VARIATION

1 Write the following on the board:

There are _____   *There are* _____
there are _____   *there are* _____
there are _____   *there are* _____
and there are _____   *and there are* _____
in the classroom I like.   *when I look out of my*
     little tent on the beach.

2 Make strips of paper bearing these words:

white curtains	beautiful kites	high waves	friendly teachers

surfboards	lots of posters	comfortable chairs	white clouds

Put the strips on the board with Blu-Tack. Ask some students to come to the board, take a strip and put it in the right gap.

3 Next, repeat steps 1 and 2 using the following prompts:

There is _____   *There is* _____
there is _____   *there is* _____
there is _____   *there is* _____
there is _____   *there is* _____
and _____   *in the town I do not like living in.*
in the film I'd like to make.

and strips bearing the following:

much noise	a sheriff	no park	a carriage

a small town	a gangster	no playground	a lot of traffic	lots of gold

Here are two texts by ten-year-old learners in the first year of English.

There is a monster,   *There are beautiful flowers,*
there are snakes,   *there is a big old tree,*
there is a castle,   *there are apples on the tree,*
there is a prince,   *there are bushes*
and there is a king   *and there is a bird*
in the story I'm going to write.   *in the picture I'm going to paint.*

1.4

GRAMMAR
Something/ anything

LEVEL
Lower intermediate +

TIME
40 minutes

EXTRAS
Handouts of a model text; realia or pictures from home; a class set of blank slips of paper

PRESENTS

Preparation

1 In the lesson before, ask students to bring a favourite present or a picture of it to the next class. You bring something too.
2 Make one photocopy of the model text for each group of four students. Cut each copy up into line by line strips.
3 Make a class set of blank slips of paper. The slips need only be big enough for students to write their names on.

Lead-in activities

The teacher's favourite present
Show your present around and/or tell your class a story based upon it. In your story, say who you got it from, where and when you got it, and also why this is one of your favourite presents.

The students' favourite presents
1 Divide the class into groups of four. One student in each group starts by showing their present, but doesn't talk about it at first. The other members of the group should speculate about the object and come up with a short background story about it. Ask them to

include in their stories who their classmate got the present from, when and where they got it and why it is a favourite.

2 The student whose present it is then tells the real story behind it.

Gift giving

1 Arrange your class in a big circle. Give everyone a pen and paper.
2 Give each student a strip of paper to write their name on.
3 Collect the strips, then hand them out again to different people.
4 Ask everyone to imagine that they are going to give a present to the student whose name they received. Give them time to think what they would give. Give a few examples (including symbolic gifts):

Monica, my present to you is a big meadow with lots of beautiful flowers and butterflies.

Michael, for you I have a magic ball. Whenever you touch it, you will hear a beautiful tune.

Tom, here is my present to you: a tiny little box. When you open it, you will find a picture in it. It is a special picture with a golden frame. The picture changes all the time and you always see in it what you want to see.

Stress that everyone must avoid judging or putting people down when giving a present. (For example, if anyone knows their partner has recently told a lie like having been unable to do homework because of a dentist appointment, they do not give *truth* as a present, instead they should choose something completely different, such as a computer that does a person's homework for them when they don't feel like doing it themselves.) If teaching teenagers, remind them to give the gift with humour and a sense of fun, not with sarcasm.

5 Everyone offers their gifts, one after the other.

Presentation of model text

1 Form groups. Give a cut-up copy of the model text to each group.
2 Ask the groups to arrange the lines so as to recreate the original.
3 When they have finished, get them to read out their texts to the class. Then read out the original for the students to check.

Model text
My birthday

For my birthday
you can give me
something to play with
or something that I can use
or something very small
but please don't give me
anything my sister might like
and don't give me anything
that is purple or pink.   © Longman Group UK Ltd 1992

Text reconstruction

1 Ask each group to lay out the strips in the order shown above.
2 Ask them to study the text carefully.
3 Collect the strips.
4 Write down the following prompts on the board. Help your learners to reconstruct the text orally. Give several learners a chance to say the whole text.

For _____
_____ give me
something _____
or _____
or _____
but please don't _____
anything_____
and don't _____

_____ .

Text creation

Ask students to write their own texts based on the model text. Display these texts in class, together with the visuals your students have brought along to class.
Here are two texts written by thirteen-year-old students:

For my birthday
you can give me
some things I can use to play with
or something like a small book,
but please don't give me
any toy cars or any dolls.

For my birthday
you can give me
a book or a game
but please don't give me an animal
or anything to eat
or anything that is very big,
because my room is very small.

Model text for adults
For my birthday
you can give me
something to read
or something to listen to
or you could take me out
to a restaurant,
but don't give me
another umbrella or purse
and, please, don't give me
anything to wear.
You know, I hate
taking things back.

YOU'D BETTER

Lead-in activities

1 Write *You'd better . . .* on the board and ask your students to finish the sentence orally. Elicit clarification of the situation given in each sentence by asking everybody *who* said their sentence and *to whom*. For example:

Student: You'd better give up smoking.
Teacher: Who said that?
Student: A girl?
Teacher: And who to?
Student: To her boyfriend.

2 Tell your class to get into groups of four. The students' task is to each write at least three sentences in three to five minutes. Each learner in turn then reads out a sentence and the others guess the situation.
3 The groups decide which of the situations are the commonest.
4 The groups report their findings to the whole class.

Presentation and reconstruction of model text

1 Present the gapped text on the board.

'You'd better w _____ h _____
you'd better p _____ m _____
a _____ at s _____
you'd better t _____ up your r _____
you'd better p _____ on a w _____ s _____',
they s _____ .
I u _____ , b _____ I d _____ c _____
and I d _____ even k _____ why not.

2 The students try to guess the missing words. Help through mime, gesture and hints like opposites, synonyms, grammatical categories, etc. Whenever a student calls out a correct word, fill it in.
3 Read the full model text out.

Model text
'You'd better work harder
you'd better pay more
attention at school
you'd better tidy up your room
you'd better put on a warm sweater',
they say.
I understand, but I don't care
and I don't even know why not.

1.5

GRAMMAR
You'd better
+ bare infinitive

LEVEL
Lower
intermediate +

TIME
40 minutes

EXTRAS
None

4 Ask your learners to study the gapped text for a minute or so. Then remove it/rub it out and ask several students to recite the full text from memory.

Text creation

1 The students write their own texts using the following skeleton. (You can, of course, change it depending on the level and age of your group.)

'You'd better_____
you'd better _____
you'd better _____
you'd better _____ ',
_____ say.
_____ understand, but _____ care
and _____ even know why not.

2 Ask some of your students to read out their texts. The rest of the class tries to guess the situation behind each text.

VARIATION
If you work with adults you may want to use the following model text.

'You'd better try harder',
that's what my boss said.
'You'd better be on time',
that's what my boss said.
'You'd better use your head',
that's what my boss said.
'You'd better be friendlier',
that's what I thought.
'I'd better be leaving',
that's what I said.

Text reconstruction

1 Split your class into two groups.
2 Read out the model text in a rhythmic way.
3 Invite everybody to chant with you.
4 Get group one to chant line one, group two to chant line two. Proceed like this with the rest of the text.

IT TOOK HIM AN HOUR ...

Preparation

Make a class set of the map below.

Lead-in activities

How long did it take them?
1 Distribute the maps (see figure 1 below).

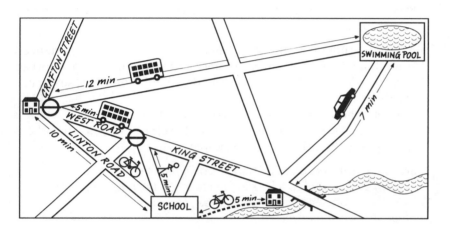

Fig. 1

2 Write 'How long did it take Sue, Tony and Sandra to get to the swimming pool after school?' on the board. Read out the following text twice.

Sue rode her bike along the river to her house. Then five minutes later, her mother took her to the swimming pool by car. Tony rode his bike to his house at the corner of Grafton Street and Linton Road and then waited 3 minutes for the bus, which he took to the swimming pool. Sandra walked to the bus stop in King Street and took the bus to the swimming pool.

3 Ask your students how long it took the three pupils to get to the pool. Read the text again if no one knows.

Reporting
1 Write the following on the board.

It took me _____ hours/days/weeks/months/
quite a long time/years to _____
It took me only _____

1.6

GRAMMAR
How long did it take you . . . ?/ him . . . ? It took him . . .

LEVEL
Lower intermediate +

TIME
50 minutes

EXTRAS
A class set of the map

2 Tell your students about something that took you quite a long time to learn, such as:

You know, when I was about six or seven I had problems figuring out what was 'right' and what was 'left'. It took me quite a long time to be able to say what was what. What helped me in the end was that I had a scar on my right hand for quite a time and so I remembered where 'right' was.

3 Then tell them about something that took you only a short time to do or learn or find out about, such as:

When I started studying at college, I realised that it was very important to be able to type. So I went to this three week course. But after a week, I knew I had already learned what I wanted to learn. So it really took me only a week to learn to type.

4 Ask your students to think of situations in which they experienced something that took quite a time and something that worked surprisingly fast. Tell them to write down not more than seven key words.

5 Get your class to work in groups of three or four.

6 Group members take turns reading out their key words. The others try to guess the situation, for example:

Student 1: smoker / give up / start again / three years
Student 2: You smoked a lot and tried to give it up, but you always started again. That was three years ago.
Student 1: No, it took me three years to stop, I don't smoke any more.

7 Each member of the class reports about another member of their group, using the following prompt (write it on the board if necessary):

I found it interesting that it (only) took
_____ (only) _____ to _____

Example:
I found it interesting that it (only) took Aiyumi (only) two years to learn as much English as she can speak now.

Presentation of model text

1 Write the first letters of each word of the model text on the board. Students guess the text. Help, if necessary, by adding more letters, giving synonyms and opposites, or by using mime or gesture.

Model text

It took him an hour
to answer my question
and it took him two days to say,
'I can't come to your party'
and a week to ring me back.
It took him six months
to write me a letter
and it will take him years
to find out
what he wants.
Phew, isn't he slow?

© Longman Group UK Ltd 1992

2 Then read the text out loud to give your students a pronunciation model. Ask them to repeat the text half out loud.

Alternatively you may hand out a copy of the model text. Ask your students to read through the text and to form mental images for each of the situations described in the text in order to facilitate memorising the model text. Then ask them to repeat the text half out loud to themselves.

Text creation

1 Write the following on the board and ask the learners to write their own texts.

It took him/her/them_____(only)

_____

Phew, isn't/aren't he/she/they slow (fast).

2 The students can then present their texts to the class. Here are two examples:

It took him a year to learn to read, and it took him eight months to understand how to work with a computer.
It also took him some weeks to finish the biology project.
It takes him days to learn a text by heart.
But it takes him only a minute to stir up a fight in our class.

It took my girlfriend only half an hour to learn to ice-skate and it took her only five minutes to learn a long text by heart.
It also took her only four days to read a book a thousand pages long and it took her only two days to learn for a difficult test.
Phew, isn't she fast!

1.7

GRAMMAR
Used to

LEVEL
Lower
intermediate +

TIME
50 minutes

EXTRAS
Cassette
recorder;
cassette of
soft, meditative
music; model
text on OHP
transparency

I USED TO DREAM

Lead-in activities

A childhood incident
Recount a pleasant episode from your childhood/adolescence, for
example:

*When I was about six, my parents and I often went to a small mountain village
for a holiday. We stayed on a farm. Close by, there was a clear stream. We
often went there and I built dams with stones and made boats from bark . . .*

A fantasy trip
1 Tell your students that you are going to take them on a fantasy trip.
Ask them to close their eyes, sit comfortably and relax. Ask them to
concentrate on their breathing for half a minute or so. Begin playing
some meditative music. When you can sense that the whole class is
relaxed, start like this:

*Imagine you are standing close to a river. It's a wonderful morning, the sun
is shining and everything is very quiet. There is a boat waiting for you. You
get in and it gently takes you down a river, slowly and gently . . . and after
some time you realise that you have been in this place before. You are back
at a time in your childhood, at a time when you were very happy. You row
to the bank of the river and get out. Walk around and take all the time you
need. You will meet all those people you spent that happy time with and
you can do all those things again that you enjoyed.*

(Pause for one or two minutes.)

*And now slowly say good-bye to the people you met and walk back to your
boat. You get into it and gently and slowly it takes you back to the place
where you stepped into it. You tie up the boat and slowly, very slowly get
out and walk up the river bank. Keep walking, take your time and return to
your chair in our classroom. When you open your eyes, you will remember
everything you saw and you will be able to tell us about the time you just
spent in your past.*

2 Allow a little time for their 'return' to the classroom. When you are
convinced that everyone is fully present, start asking your students
questions about the situations they experienced. Avoid any
impression of being nosey. If you feel that a student doesn't want to
share, ask someone else. Usually most people are willing to talk
about what they saw and felt, for example:

Student: I went for a picnic with my older sister and her boyfriend.
Teacher: Was it spring, or summer or autumn?
Student: Early summer, I think.
Teacher: Did you often go on picnics with your sister and her boyfriend?
Student: (laughing) Yes, I think my mother wanted me to go.

Thinking back

1 Give the class a minute or two to think back again to a happy time in their childhood.

2 Write *I used to . . .* on the board and ask each student to say a sentence relating to this childhood time. For example:

I used to go hiking with my father a lot.
I used to help my gran in the garden.
I used to drive a tractor when I was only ten.

3 Correct the students' sentences if necessary.

4 Ask everyone to repeat someone else's sentence. Suggest they choose the sentence they liked best.

Presentation of model text

1 Present the text below on the OHP in the following way. Show your students the first line for about two seconds. Cover the line up and ask them to write it down. Proceed sentence by sentence. Allow about twenty seconds for the writing of each line.

2 Everyone checks with a neighbour and corrects any mistakes they notice.

3 Two or three students then read their texts out. Show them the text on the OHP for final correction.

Model text (for young learners)
I used to dream of expensive clothes
I used to dream of a holiday in Hawaii
I used to dream of a Porsche
and of parties under a silvery moon
but all I want right now
is a friend
who will listen to me.

Text creation

1 Write the following prompts on the board and tell your class that they can use *He*, *She* or *They* instead of *I*.

I used to dream _____
I used to dream _____
I used to dream _____
and of _____
but all I want right now
is _____

_____

2 The students write their own texts according to the model. Afterwards, ask four or five students to read out their texts.

The following two texts, written by fourteen-year-olds, very clearly reflect their concerns and problems at the time.

He used to dream of cars
he used to dream of computers
and he used to dream
of radios and television sets
but all he wants right now
is a family
who will listen to him.

I used to dream of birthday parties
I used to dream of going out until
twelve o'clock
I used to dream of holidays in Italy
and I used to dream of being a
champion at squash,
but all I want right right now
is to be healthy.

The following text was written by an advanced student:

He used to dream of equality
he used to dream of prosperity for all
he used to dream of being admired by his people
and he used to dream of being remembered
a thousand years after his death.
But all it really needed
were courageous citizens
who toppled him from his throne.

VARIATION
If you work with adults you may want to use the following model text:

She used to dream
of a loving partner
she used to dream
of a man who would really listen to her
she used to dream
of going places
and of a never-ending dream time
together,
but all she wants right now
is someone to help with the washing up.

ACKNOWLEDGEMENTS
We adapted the fantasy trip from *The Possible Human* (Houston 1982).

I'D RATHER BE

Lead-in activity

Vocabulary work
1 Form groups of three or four.
2 On the board, write the following pairs of words:

knife - string	*apple - worm*
flag - pole	*candy - wrapper*
dictionary - word	*truck - hedgehog*
star - sky	

3 Ask each group to write down another fifteen pairs and to make one copy of their list.
4 Then ask them to pass one of their lists on, so that finally each group has two lists (their own and one from another group).

Presentation of model text

1 Fix a few copies of the model text on the walls round the class.

Model text
I'd rather be the sea than a ship
I'd rather be a kite than a plane
I'd rather be a path than a road
I'd rather be a cup than a plate
Yes I would
If I could.

© Longman Group UK Ltd 1992

2 Get your learners to stand up and go to one of the copies of the text. Tell them to memorise as much of it as possible.
3 Ask them to go back to their desks and individually note down the first line (or however much they can remember) of the text. Then they return to the text and try to memorise the next bit and so on.

Text creation

1 Ask your students to produce their own texts in groups, using the words from their two lists of word pairs. Ask them to follow the structure of the text they recently noted down.
2 One member of each group then presents their text to the class.

VARIATION
1 Write the following on the board:

soft against hard / light against dark/
warm against cool / hot against cold/
individual against whole / nature against man made things

1.8

GRAMMAR
I'd rather be . . .
than . . .

LEVEL
Lower
intermediate +

TIME
40 minutes

EXTRAS
A few copies of
the model text

Give one or two examples for each pair:

cushion - brick / sun - night /
summer - winter / fire - ice /
flower - meadow / tree - house /

2 Ask everyone to write another text either using images from one pair only (eg. soft against hard) or using images from various pairs. If your group is fairly creative, suggest trying for a humorous text that rhymes. For example:

I'd rather be a seesaw than a cat
I'd rather be a horseshoe than a hat
I'd rather be a coat rack than a mat
I'd rather be a monster than a bat
Yes I would
If I could.

The following was written by a thirteen-year-old:

I'd rather be the sun than the moon
I'd rather be a pearl than an oyster
I'd rather be a ring than a finger
I'd rather be an angel than a devil
Yes, I would
If I could.

1.9

GRAMMAR
Superlatives

LEVEL
Elementary –
lower
intermediate

TIME
30 minutes

EXTRAS
Class sets of
words handouts;
(optional) model
text on OHP
transparency; a
few bilingual
dictionaries

I'D LIKE TO BE

Lead-in activities

Noun study

1 Hand out a copy of the following words to each of your students and allow them fifteen seconds to study it.

butterfly	snowman	rainbow	snowflake
sports car	helicopter	pizza	pilot
teacher	tiger	elephant	piano
mineral	diamond ring	wind	eagle
friend	flower	insect	knife
river	pudding	ice cream	policeman
leaf	fairy	witch	snake
ball	tennis racket	storybook	word
shark	rainbow	surfboard	cheesecake

© Longman Group UK Ltd 1992

2 Ask them to put their papers face down on their desks.

Noun collection
1 In pairs students write down as many of the words as they can remember. Allow about two minutes for this.
2 Ask them to shout out the words. Write them on the board.

Associations and dissociations
1 Ask each pair to choose one noun from the list and note down at least three adjectives that they associate with it plus at least one adjective they think has nothing at all to do with it. Give a few examples:

ball: red, big, lovely (associations) / stupid (disassociation)

2 Ask pairs to read out their words. Note them on the board in two different colours.

Comparatives and superlatives
1 Next comes a quick response exercise. One student starts by calling out a classmate's name and one of the adjectives from the board.
2 The student called has to quickly say the comparative and the superlative. If right, erase that adjective from the board. If not, leave it until someone else gets both the comparative and superlative correct.
3 Continue until all the adjectives on the board have been erased.

Presentation of model text

Display the following on OHP or poster paper.

Model text
The most colourful butterfly
The sweetest cheesecake
The most beautiful tiger
The smallest snowflake
The fattest caterpillar
and the most dangerous snowman.
These are what I would like to be.

Text creation

Students write their own texts using bilingual dictionaries.
The following text was written by a twelve-year-old in her second year of learning English.

The most expensive ring,
the softest teddy bear,
the nicest rainbow,
the most colourful surfboard,
the biggest pizza
and the nicest teacher.
These are what I would like to be.

1.10

GRAMMAR
Comparisons,
*look good/smell
good*

LEVEL
Lower
intermediate +

TIME
50 minutes

EXTRAS
A recording of
soft, meditative
music

AREN'T I LOVELY?

Lead-in activities

Word collection

1 Write the following on the board:
   I'm very, very lovely?   *strawberry*

2 Ask your students to give you as many words as they can think of that go with either of these two stimuli. Ask your students to shout words to you, ask which stimulus they belong to and write the words in a halo around each stimulus.

Focus on poems

1 Read out the poems A and B (below).

2 Ask everyone to close their eyes and listen as you read the poems a second time. Depending on the level of your class, you may want to explain some vocabulary beforehand. When we tried out the activity with twelve-year-olds in their second year of English, we pre-taught *leaves, dropped, freeze, soup tureen* and *lima bean*.

   When working with adults, we asked them to do a short visualisation exercise before we read out the poems:

   'Close your eyes and imagine you are standing in front of a mirror . . . go closer and look into it . . . now you realise that you're getting younger and younger until you are about ten or twelve. Take your time and look very carefully at your reflection and then slowly, slowly step back from the mirror, say good-bye to your image and return to the here and now of our classroom.'

3 When you have finished, allow some seconds of silence for the poems to echo in the students' minds.

4 Then read them out again to a background of soft, meditative music.

Poem A	Poem B
ME	*I liked growing.*
My nose is blue,	*That was nice.*
My teeth are green,	*The leaves were soft*
My face is like a soup tureen.	*The sun was hot.*
I look just like a lima bean.	*I was warm and red and round*
I'm very, very lovely.	*Then someone dropped me in a pot.*
My feet are far too short	*Being a strawberry isn't all pleasing.*
And long.	*This morning they put me into ice cream.*
My hands are left and right	*I'm freezing.*
And wrong.	
My voice is like the hippo's song.	
I'm very, very,	
Very, very,	
Very, very	
Lovely?	

(Both poems by Karla Kuskin, *Dogs and Dragons/Trees and Dreams*, Harper and Row 1980)

5 Ask your students to call out more words for noting down on the board. Some will come up with words they remember from your reading, others may well suggest new words.

Dictogloss

1 Tell your students that you are going to give them a dictation, but they are not allowed to note anything down before you have finished it. Tell them that you are going to read the text just twice. Their task – immediately after each dictation – is to jot down whatever they can remember, then get together with a partner and try to reconstruct the text. Allow about three minutes.

2 The students dictate the text back to you. You write it on the board. If no one gives the right wording or if the students' suggestions contain grammatical errors, elicit words and correct forms with mime and gesture. If you get more than one suggestion and all are equally good, say that all are possible but try to elicit the original word or form.

Dictogloss text

My earlobe is bigger than a strawberry,
my nose is longer than a carrot,
my feet are shorter than potatoes,
my hair is thicker than grass,
my fingers are like beans,
I look good
I smell good
– no wonder everybody likes me.

Text reconstruction

1 Ask everyone to close their eyes.
2 Erase certain words from the text you have on the board (see Skeleton text below).
3 Tell them to open their eyes and give you the missing words. Continue until they have reconstructed the text.

Skeleton text

My_____ _____ _____ than _____ _____ ,
my_____ _____ _____ than _____ _____ ,
my_____ _____ _____ than _____ ,
my_____ _____ _____ than _____ ,
my_____ _____ like _____ ,
I _____ _____
I _____ _____
no wonder _____ _____ _____ .

Text creation

1 Before you ask the students to create their own texts, you may want to collect and/or introduce words under the following headings: *parts of the body, adjectives, fruit, vegetables.*

2 Tell your students that they can also use *his* or *her* instead of *my* and that they need not stick to the topic area of the model text. They can also write about other topic areas such as 'my room', 'our class-room', 'my garden' or 'my pet'.

The following example was written by a twelve-year-old.

My head is bigger than a pumpkin.
My ears are bigger than a tennis ball.
My teeth are blacker than a chimney
sweep.
My shoes are bigger than an elephant's
feet.
My nose is thinner than asparagus.
My hair is bluer than the sky.
I look happy,
I look sad,
no wonder I'm the clown.

ACKNOWLEDGEMENT
The dictogloss seems to have first been described in *The ELT Journal* in 1963. We first encountered it in *Dictation* (Davis and Rinvolucri 1988, p.70).

1.11

GRAMMAR
Negative + *want*
somebody to . . .

LEVEL
Intermediate +

TIME
50 – 60 minutes

EXTRAS
(Optional) OHP
or big flash poster
or stiff cards

I DON'T WANT HER TO . . .

Preparation

Write phrases (below) on an OHP transparency, a big flash poster or stiff cards.

Lead-in activities

What I don't want
1 Ask your students to work in groups of three to five.
2 Give groups the following instructions.

Group A
You are younger brothers or sisters. Your older brothers or sisters often tell you to do things you don't like. What I want you to do is to write as many sentences as possible of the pattern, I don't want them to . . . .
For example: I don't want her/him/them to tell me that I am not old enough to do something.

Group B

You are parents. Write down what you don't want your children to do.
Your model sentence is, We don't want you to . . . .
For example: We don't want you to get home later than ten.

Group C

You are children. Write down what you don't want your parents to do.
Your model sentence is, I don't want them to . . . .
For example: I don't want them to tell me how much money they spend on me.

If you teach a large class, here are some more ideas for groups D and E.

Group D

You are an employer/a teacher. Think about your employees/students.
Your model sentence is, I don't want you to . . . .
For example: I don't want you to be late.

Group E

You are employees/students. Referring to your boss/teacher your model sentence is, I don't want him/her to . . . .
For example: I don't want him/her to make jokes about the mistakes I make.

3 When the groups have finished, collect what they have written, read out individual sentences and ask the groups to guess who the speakers are (eg. boss/parents).

Look and remember

1 Show the following phrases very briefly to your learners. Tell them not to write anything down at this stage. (Concentration is often highest when the students know that they have only a limited amount of time to study the words.) Ideally show the phrases on an OHP and simply switch it off after a short period of time. Otherwise, use a big flash poster or stiff cards with the words on them.

Be polite	*work harder.*
Don't tell me to	*my things without asking.*
Don't use	*you feel like it.*
Interrupt me whenever	*to call me names.*
I don't want him	*than me.*
She is older	*please.*

2 Individually the students write down as many phrases as they can remember and then pool their notes with a partner.
3 Ask them to repeat the chunks of language back to you while you copy them on the board.
4 Ask them to decide which phrases go together. Connect them by drawing lines on the board.

Presentation of model text

Model text
*All right
she is two years older than me
but I don't want her to
call me 'little one',
I don't want her to
interrupt me
whenever she feels like it,
I don't want her to
use my things without asking
and I don't want her to
tell me to be polite.
Let her change first.*

1 Write the first letters of each word of the model text on the board or on a poster. The length of the gaps should correspond roughly to the length of the words that fit in them. This will not only facilitate the students' guesswork, but will also make your board work neater. Invite students to guess the words. For example:
   *A__ r____
   s __ i_ t __ y ____ o ____ t ___ m _*

2 When you have elicited the text, read it out again.
3 Before your students write their own texts you might want to elicit individual sentences and write them on the board/OHP. In the writing to follow, the pool of sentences below can serve as a source of ideas and phrases. For example:

   *I don't want him to listen to my cassettes.
   I don't want them to check my exercise books.
   I don't want her to buy pink nighties for me.*

Text creation

Ask your students to write their own texts. Prompt, if necessary:
*All right
he is . . . / they are/my parents . . ./ she is six years younger than me . . . .*

The following texts are by students in their fourth year of English.

*All right
she is my teacher,
but I don't want her to give me
such a lot of homework.
I don't want her to interrupt me
all the time.
And I don't want her to ask me
words that I don't know.
But otherwise she is O.K.*

*All right
they are my parents,
but I don't want them to come
into my room without asking,
I don't want them to read my letters,
I don't want them to laugh
at my friends,
I don't want them to check my homework,
all I want is to live my own life.*

VARIATION

If you work with adults, you may want to use the following text:

All right
he's my boyfriend,
but I don't want him to
slurp his soup
I don't want him to
wear pink ties with polka dots
and I really don't want him to go on saying
'That's what my mother says'.
I want him to
buy some anti-dandruff shampoo
I want him to
use a different aftershave
and unless he does – that's it.

DO YOU REALLY MIND HIM BITING HIS NAILS?

Lead-in activities

Make up your mind
1 Present the following list:

Some people . . .
talk about themselves all the time
don't listen when you talk to them
drive agressively
never admit mistakes
have bad breath
bite their nails
make a noise by tapping their biro while you're talking to them
lose their things all the time
leave their things lying around
pick their nose in public
never keep appointments on time
don't keep promises
forget what has been agreed on
gossip a lot
smoke during meals
eat noisily
talk with their mouths full
are very fussy about their food
talk on the phone for ages
play music very loud on the beach/in the street
worry a lot

1.12

GRAMMAR
Do you mind +
object + *-ing*

LEVEL
Intermediate +

TIME
60 minutes

EXTRAS
Class set of
handouts of
skeleton text

never look into your eyes when talking to you
wear dirty clothes
don't wash their hair regularly
use rude language
make dirty jokes
boast a lot
don't write legibly
make very clear that they feel very important
put themselves down all the time

2 Tell your students to write down five things from the list under the heading *It annoys me if someone . . .* and five things under the heading *I don't mind people . . . ing . . . .* Give one or two examples for each list.

Group work
1 Ask your students to discuss in groups of four what they find annoying and why, and also what things they don't mind. Get them to add whatever else they think should be in the list.
2 Ask each group to decide which three things they find most annoying of all. Allow time to reach a group consensus.
3 Ask a representative to report the group consensus to the class.
4 Ask if there is anybody who doesn't mind the behaviour that others find very annoying. If there are students who don't mind certain things, ask them for their reasons. For example:

Student 1: I don't mind people who are fussy about their food.
Teacher: Why's that?
Student 1: Because they might be on a diet or maybe they don't eat
*   certain things for religious reasons.*

Presentation and reconstruction of model text

Hand out copies of the following skeleton texts and ask your students to try to fill them in.

Skeleton text A
D_ y_ _ r_ _ _ _ _ m_ _ _ m_ s_ _ _ _ _ _ _ e_ _ _ _ S_ _ _ _ _ _ _
a_ a f_ _ _ _ _ _ _ m_ _ _ _?
D_ y_ _ r_ _ _ _ _ m_ _ _ m_ s_ _ _ _ _ _ _ t_ _ e_ _ _ _ _ _ _
t_ _ _ _ _ _ _ _ w_ _ _ m_ m_ _ _ _ b_ _ _?
D_ y_ _ r_ _ _ _ _ m_ _ _ m_ s_ _ _ _ _ _ l_ _ _ a c_ _ _ _ _ _ _?
D_ y_ _ r_ _ _ _ _ m_ _ _ m_ g_ _ _ _ _ _ d_ _ _ _ o_ _ _ i_ a
w_ _ _ _?
W_ _ _ , t_ _ _ w_'_ _ h_ _ _ t_ s_ _ g_ _ _-b_ _ b_ _ _ _ _ _
I d_ m_ _ _ i_ _ _ _ _ _ _ _ p_ _ _ _ _ .

Skeleton text B

D _ y _ _ r _ _ _ _ _ m _ _ _ m _ b _ _ _ _ l _ _ _ o _ _ _ i _ a
w _ _ _ _ ?
D _ y _ _ r _ _ _ _ _ m _ _ _ m _ f _ _ _ _ _ _ _ _ _ m _ h _ _ _ _ _ _ _ ?
D _ y _ _ r _ _ _ _ _ m _ _ _ m _ t _ _ _ _ _ _ t _ m _ m _ _ _ _
w _ _ _ I' _ b _ _ _ _ ?
D _ y _ _ r _ _ _ _ _ m _ _ _ m _ s _ _ _ _ _ _ _ i _ t _ _ t _ _ _ _ _ ?
D _ y _ _ r _ _ _ _ _ m _ _ _ m _ s _ _ _ _ _ _ _ l _ _ _ _ _ _ ?
W _ _ _ , t _ _ _ w _ ' _ _ h _ _ _ t _ s _ _ g _ _ _ -b _ _ b _ _ _ _ _ _
I d _ m _ _ _ n _ _ _ _ _ -m _ _ _ _ _ t _ _ _ _ _ _ _ .

© Longman Group UK Ltd 1992

Text A (key)

Do you really mind me spending every Saturday at a football match?
Do you really mind me spending the evenings tinkering with my motor bike?
Do you really mind me smoking like a chimney?
Do you really mind me getting drunk once in a while?
Well, then we'll have to say good-bye because
I do mind intolerant people.

Text B (key)

Do you really mind my being late once in a while?
Do you really mind my forgetting my homework?
Do you really mind my talking to my mates when I'm bored?
Do you really mind my smoking in the toilet?
Do you really mind my skipping lessons?
Well, then we'll have to say good-bye because
I do mind narrow-minded teachers.

VARIATION

Write the texts on the board or on an OHP transparency. Avoid slackening the pace during the guessing process by giving more letters of the word to guess; by providing words that roughly mean the same; by using mime and gesture.

Text creation

The students write their own texts and then read them out loud or display them in the classroom.

1.13

GRAMMAR
To have a try at . . .-ing

LEVEL
Intermediate +

TIME
30 minutes

EXTRAS
Class set of
worksheet

I'D LOVE TO HAVE A TRY AT LEARNING JAPANESE

Lead-in activities

Things we'd love to have a try at
1 Raise the issue of things people would like to do but never get around to doing. Give one or two personal examples.
2 On the board/OHP write a short list of sentences referring to activities suitable for the age of your students. For example:

I'd love to have a try at playing golf.
I'd love to have a try at making a video film.
I'd love to have a try at learning to dance / to cook / a foreign language.

3 Ask students to note down two things they would love to try doing.
4 Invite them to read their sentences out. Ask whether they think they will actually do these things. Move on to eliciting more general ideas of why some people never fulfil their dreams.

Presentation of model text

Read out the following text twice.

'I'd love to have a try at playing squash,
I'd love to have a try at doing jazz dance,
I'd love to have a try at cross-country skiing,
I'd love to have a try at judo,'
he said.
But he never had the time
because he spent all his time watching sport on TV.

Text creation

1 Hand out copies of the worksheet. Ask your students to write their own texts individually or in pairs. Encourage them to mention activities additional to those on the worksheet.
2 Ask individual students or pairs to read out their texts.

WORKSHEET

'I'd love to have a try at *learning to . . .'*
taking part in . . .'
writing a book . . .'
building a . . .'
opening a . . .'
selling . . .'

he / she / my friend / my father / my uncle / my sister / my boss / . . . said.
But he/she never . . .
Because he/she . . .

© Longman Group UK Ltd 1992

IT'S TOO HOT

Lead-in activities

Carry out instructions

Choose a student and ask him/her to carry out (not merely mime) an action. Do this several times, sometimes using new vocabulary for actions. Mime the action if a student does not understand the vocabulary. (Your class will have more fun if some of your instructions are unexpected or unusual.) For example:

Maria, go to the board.
(Maria goes to the board)
Take a piece of blue chalk.
(She takes a piece of blue chalk)
Draw a circle.
(She draws a circle)
Thank you, Maria, sit down.
(She sits down).

Francoise, come up front.
(She comes out etc.)
Take a piece of red chalk.
Put it in your left hand.
Draw a mouth in the circle.

Here is a routine we have used with seven-year-old-children in one of their very first EFL classes, much to their enjoyment.

Take your pencil case.
Put it on your head.
Stand up.
Hands up.
Hands down.
Turn round.
Look down and catch it.

Depending on the level of your learners, they might enjoy preparing their own instructions individually or in small groups and then giving them to a partner.

Presentation of model text

1 Display or hand out copies of the following model text to your learners. Say each item and mime the action for each one.
2 Repeat. This time ask your learners to do the actions with you.

Model text
Drink it up
It's too hot
Carry it home

1.14

GRAMMAR
Too + adjective, imperatives

LEVEL
Elementary

TIME
30 – 50 minutes

EXTRAS
(Optional) Class set of model text

It's too heavy
Write it down
It's too difficult
Take it off
It's too cold
Put it on
It's too tight.

© Longman Group UK Ltd 1992

3 Repeat the text as a chant with the whole class.
4 Divide your class in two groups and get each group to chant every other line rhythmically.

Group A: Drink it up.
Group B: It's too hot.
Group C: Carry it home.   *etc.*

Text reconstruction

1 Elicit the model text from your class by silently miming.
2 Lead a choral repetition of the text from memory. If the class get stuck or make mistakes, do not give them the language straight away. Use mime, gesture and key words to aid them.

Text creation

1 If you think your class will need prompts, put a list of actions and a list of adjectives on the board, for example:

Actions
Open	*the window*
	the door
	your schoolbag
	your mouth
	your eyes
Shut	*the window*
	the door
	your schoolbag
Buy	*a watch*
	some tea
Put on	*your hat*
Take off	*your coat*
Switch	*on* *the light*
	off
Pick up	*your bag*
	the ball

Adjectives
boring, funny, cold, hot, young, old, small, narrow, big, heavy, light,
dark, bright, draughty, expensive, cheap, stuffy, full

2 Ask your students to create their own texts based on the model text.
3 Ask individual students to read out the texts they have created
while the rest of the class mimes the actions.

ACKNOWLEDGEMENTS
This lesson is in the tradition of Total Physical Response, a method
developed by James Asher. You can get a good idea of how to work
with TPR from his book *Learning Another Language Through Actions:*
The Complete Language Teacher's Guidebook (1986).

The example, *Take your pencil case . . .*, comes from our coursebook
for teaching English as a foreign language to primary school children,
Conrad and Company by Ballinger, Gerngross, Hladnig, Puchta (1991).

Carolyn Graham's books (1978 and 1979) are an excellent source of
jazz chants, some of which lend themselves well to TPR lessons.

SHE FELT LIKE . . .

Lead-in activities

Match the parts
1 Write *I felt like* . . . on the board and in a box give the students
possible endings as in figure 2. Tailor the endings you give to the
language that you have taught so far.

> *hiding in a hole – slapping his/her face –*
> *having a huge meal – hugging him/her*
> *– running away – saying 'No' – saying I was sorry –*
> *joining him/her – offering him/her a drink*
> *– smiling – bursting out laughing –*
> *saying 'That was the last time . . . '*

Fig.2

2 Give the students a series of sentence beginnings by dictation, by
writing on the board, etc. For example:
When he / she read out the poem . . .
When he / she asked me that stupid question . . .
When he / she stopped crying . . .
When he / she called me an idiot . . .

3 Ask them to finish these sentence starters by adding first *I felt like*
and then an ending from the box (orally or in writing).

1.15

GRAMMAR
. . . felt like . . . -ing

LEVEL
Intermediate +

TIME
50 minutes

EXTRAS
A skeleton of the
model text on
OHP transparency
or poster paper,
two slips of paper
for each student

Make your choice
1 Clear your prompts off the board.
2 Ask everyone to repeat the one sentence they liked best. It does not matter if several students give the same sentence.

Make your own sentence
1 Each student writes a new sentence following the same pattern on two slips of paper, for example:

> *When she asked me not to phone her any more,*

> *I felt like smashing the receiver.*

2 First collect the slips that start with *When* . . . and then the ones starting with *I felt* . . .. Keep the stacks separate.
3 Hand them out to your students again so that each student gets one slip from each stack.
4 One after the other the students read out their slips starting with *When* . . .. The others suggest possible endings. If no one suggests the original ending, the student who wrote it says what it was.

Presentation and reconstruction of model text

1 Display a skeleton version of the model text, which gives only the first letter of each word.

Model text
When she opened the window,
she felt like throwing gold-dust all over the buildings.
When she listened to the cars in the street ,
she felt like turning them into panthers.
When she looked at her tiny garden,
she felt like changing it into a jungle.
And when she looked at herself in the mirror,
she felt like painting her face the
colours of the rainbow.

2 Ask the students to reconstruct the text. Help them by offering synonyms, opposites and by using mime, gesture, etc.
3 When they have reconstructed the text, ask your students to close their eyes. Read the text out to round things off.

Text creation

Students write their own texts. You might want to provide the following prompts on the board:

When ___ ___ ,
___ felt like ___ ing ___ ,
When ___ ___ ,
___ felt like ___ ing ___

____

1.16

GRAMMAR
Hear/see + object
+ bare infinitive

LEVEL
Lower
intermediate +

TIME
40 minutes

EXTRAS
Class set of comic
strip handout
overleaf

I SAW A CHICKEN KICK A LAMP-POST

Lead-in activities

Collect words

1 Write *people, animals, things, actions* as headings on the board. Elicit a couple of examples for each category (*fireman, horse, calendar, to eat,* etc.) and write them in columns under the headings.
2 Ask your students to extend each column. Allow three to five minutes for them to do this on paper.
3 Ask them for their words and add them onto the board.

Mime the action

1 Ask everyone to stand up and to carry out the following actions: *light a candle, brush your teeth, kick the ball, throw the dice, put on a hat, climb a palm tree,* etc.
2 They sit down and write two more actions on paper using the words from their lists.
3 Get the class to stand up in a circle. One after the other, students tell the class to mime the actions they have written down. (Or, each student mimes his or her actions and the others guess them.)
4 Hand out copies of the comic strip overleaf (figure 3). Tell your class to describe the frames of the comic strip using the following pattern: *I saw a ladder dance rock'n'roll.*
5 Each student reads their sentences out to the class.

NOTE
We found that both adult and younger learners were more attracted by a surreal model sentence like the one above, as opposed to something like *I saw my friend work at his computer.*

Fig. 3

Presentation of model text

Read out the model text. As you read the last two lines, conspicuously cross your fingers.

Model text
I saw a chicken kick a lamp-post
I saw a cactus drive a car
I heard a penguin eat spaghetti
I saw a teacher break a window
I heard a policeman howl at the moon
I saw a tree jump over a fence
and I swear it is true
John saw it too.

Text creation

1 The students write their own texts in pairs. For 'John' each substitutes their partner's name.
2 Text publication (see page 8).

NOTE
Depending on the level of your group, you might want to explain when the bare infinitive (instead of the *-ing* form) is used after *see* and *hear*. 'We use an infinitive after *hear* and *see* to say that we heard or saw the whole of an action or event . . .' (Swan 1980, p.289).

WHAT'S PINK?

1.17

GRAMMAR
's / of

LEVEL
Elementary –
intermediate

TIME
30 – 40 minutes

EXTRAS
Class set of
worksheets
A, B and C

Lead-in activity

A guessing game
1 Tell your students that you are thinking of something red. Ask them to guess what it is. Allow only questions to which the answer can either be 'yes' or 'no'.
2 The student who guesses correctly continues: *I'm thinking of something green* (or blue, etc.).

Presentation of model text

1 Hand out copies of worksheet A or write the texts on the board.
2 Ask your students to fill in the gaps in text A.
3 Have them read out their solutions.
4 After that, read out the text twice.
5 Proceed in the same way using text B.

WORKSHEET A
Text A
What's purple?
My sister's _____
my father's _____
the _____ of my _____
my new _____
and the _____
I'm not _____ to _____
on my _____ .

car	hair	allowed	eyeshade	use	cover
	jeans	diary	dye		

Text B
What's blue?
The _____ and the ocean
our maths teacher's _____
the _____ of the fly
that _____ my _____
and the paper of your _____
I _____ in my _____ drawer.

secret	nose	body	keep	letter	sky
	head	circles			

Model text A
What's purple?
My sister's eyeshade
my father's car
the cover of my diary
my new jeans
and the dye
I'm not allowed to use
on my hair.

Model text B
What's blue?
The sky and the ocean
our maths teacher's nose
the body of the fly
that circles my head
and the paper of your letter
I keep in my secret drawer.

Presentation of another model text

1 Form pairs.
2 Student A gets Worksheet B and student B Worksheet C. Student A dictates to B the words B needs and vice versa. They are not, however, allowed to look at their partner's worksheet.
3 When they have finished the dictation, they compare their texts.

WORKSHEET B
Text C
What's pink?
Strawberry ——————
the _____
I _____ *for* _____ *birthday*
my _____ *friend's* _____
and _____ *cuddly* _____
who _____ *me*
when _____ *am* _____

WORKSHEET C
Text C
What's pink?
_____ *ice cream*
_____ *cake*
_____ *had* _____ *my* _____
_____ *best* _____ *earrings*
_____ *the* _____ *mouse*
_____ *watches* _____
_____ *I* _____ *asleep.*

© Longman Group UK Ltd 1992

Model text C
What's pink?
Strawberry ice cream
the cake
I had for my birthday
my best friend's earrings
and the cuddly mouse

who watches me
when I am asleep.

Text creation

1 Read out model texts A, B and C again. Before you read, ask your students to close their eyes and picture all the things you are reading about.
2 Ask them which text they like best. Encourage them to give reasons for their choice .
3 Then tell them to choose a colour and write their own text.
4 When they have finished, tell them to stick their texts on the walls of the classroom.
5 Every student should read as many texts as possible and give feedback if they like a certain text. If necessary, put up two or three posters with language they might need for this, for example:

I like your text because ...
Your text reminds me of ...
I really enjoyed reading your text.
I think your text is great.
It's a beautiful text.
I wish I could write such a text.
When I read your text I thought of ...
I'd like to have a copy of your text.
Your text made me feel happy/sad ...

NOTE
Although designed for elementary students, intermediate learners have also enjoyed this activity. Here is a text from an intermediate class.

What's black?
The frozen leg
of the soldier,
the burnt tree,
the seabird in the oil slick,
the river of poison
and the mushroom cloud
in the sky.

1.18

GRAMMAR
Adjectives/
adverbs

LEVEL
Lower
intermediate

TIME
50 minutes

EXTRAS
(Optional) A sheet
of poster paper for
text A; (optional)
flash cards; one
copy of jumbled
text B per group of
four; OHP trans-
parency or flash
cards of text C; class
set of gapped text D

HE COOKS WELL AND HIS FOOD SMELLS VERY GOOD

Preparation

1 Copy a version of text A – in which only the first letters of each word are given – on OHP transparency (or poster paper).
2 Copy text C onto OHP transparency or flashcards (one line per card).

Presentation of text A

1 Read out text A three times. The first time, your students just listen. During the second reading they mime the actions with you. For the third reading they close their eyes and try to picture the situation. After the third reading, ask them questions about the person's appearance.

Text A
He plays the guitar beautifully
He dances well
He moves fast
He sings well
There is just one problem:
nobody listens.

2 Present text A (on poster paper or OHP). Remove the text after a minute. Ask your students to work in pairs and reconstruct the text.

Presentation of text B

1 Form groups of four. Read out text B. Ask your students to listen while you mime the actions.
2 Tell them to close their eyes and visualise the situation while you read the text a second time.
3 Hand out copies of a jumbled version of the text. Ask the groups to put the sentences into the correct order.
4 When students have assembled the text, read your original again as a check.

Model text B
The big car moved silently down the road.
I quickly hid behind the bushes.
The car stopped and a man slowly got out.
The doorbell of the dark house rang loudly.
A man and a woman started to talk angrily.
Then a shot rang out suddenly.
I saw the man's hat gently rolling away.

Jumbled text B
The doorbell of the dark house rang loudly.
I saw the man's hat gently rolling away.
The car stopped and a man slowly got out.
The big car moved silently down the road.
Then a shot rang out suddenly.
I quickly hid behind the bushes.
A man and a woman started to talk angrily.

© Longman Group UK Ltd 1992

Presentation of text C

1 Show your students each line of text C very briefly (on OHP or flash cards). Their task is to write each line down.
2 When they have finished, they check with their neighbours. Allow two minutes for this.
3 Read out the text twice. Then show it on the OHP (or display all your flash cards).

Text C
It smells good
It tastes great
It looks beautiful
It feels soft
It's my latest recipe:
Strawberry cake.

Presentation of text D

1 Form pairs. Hand out copies of gapped text D.
2 When your students have filled in the gaps, they read out their solutions.
3 Finally, read out the model text.

Gapped text D
It looks _____
It smells _____
It feels _____
_____ *what it is:*
My _____ *dog.*

| little | wonderful | guess | marvellous | good |

© Longman Group UK Ltd 1992

Text D
It looks wonderful
It smells good
It feels marvellous
Guess what it is?
My little dog.

Distinguishing between adjectives and adverbs

1 Draw the following grid and write in some adjectives and adverbs .

ADJECTIVE	ADVERB
good	beautifully
wonderful	fast

2 Read texts A – D out again and tell your students to shout 'Stop' when they think you've just read out an adjective or an adverb. As adjectives and adverbs are identified, write them down under the correct heading on the board. Ask students to write down from memory the sentence they like best. It must, however, contain one of the words from the grid.
3 Students read out their sentences.

Text creation

Now ask your students to create their own texts individually or in pairs. You may want to give them another example.

Text E
He chews slowly
He eats noisily
but he cooks well
and his food smells very, very good.

1.19

GRAMMAR
Gerund after
prepositions

LEVEL
Intermediate +

TIME
60 – 80 minutes

EXTRAS
(Optional) class
set of text C
handout

OLD TRAPS

The activity is not suitable for learners below the age of 15. Additionally, there should be a strong bond of trust among the members of the group. (For exercises to build trust in the language classroom, see Moskowitz 1978 and Davis and Rinvolucri 1990.)

Lead-in activities

Nina
1 Read out text A.
2 Ask everyone to close their eyes and imagine what Nina looks like as you read the text again.
3 Invite your students to say what came to mind.

Text A
Nina, who is in her first year of college, decides to spend her Christmas vaca-
tion with her family, although it is hard for her to leave her boyfriend Mitch.

She examined herself in mirrors all over the house: the speckled mirror in the
bathroom, the little oval mirror in the upstairs hall, the long narrow glass over
her parents' bulky, old-fashioned bureau. In every mirror she saw only herself.
Nina Pudding Face. Her old disparaging name for herself, popped out like a
jack-in-the-box. Wasn't it awful? Without Mitch at her elbow to tell her that
he loved her, she fell right back into that old trap of disliking herself.

Norma Fox Mazer, *Someone to Love*, Delacorte Press 1985 p.133

The teacher's story
Tell a story about a time you felt small or unworthy because of something somebody else said, for example:

A long time ago when I was a student, I took part in an English language
workshop over the weekend for rather advanced learners. We were sitting in
a circle and the teacher was just about to begin, having introduced himself in
a slight Northern accent. At that moment, a stocky man in his fifties, with
glasses and wearing a suit asked, 'Is it Queen's English we are going to use in
our conversation?' Our teacher was kind of startled and didn't quite know
what to say. The effect of the man's sentence on the rest of the group was,
however, devastating. Everybody seemed to be asking themselves whether
the workshop was the right thing for them. I clearly remember feeling very
bad about the level of my English and praying that the teacher would not pair
me up with the man who had spoken. I later found out that most of the other
participants had had the same feeling. We were very relieved when the man
left after a couple of hours.

The students' stories
1 Form groups of four.
2 Everyone thinks back to a situation in which they, or somebody else
   they know very well, felt small, miserable or unworthy because of
   something somebody else had said. They all take notes and then tell
   their stories in the group.

Presentation of model text

1 Write Gapped text B on the board and elicit the complete words.

Gapped text B
It was awful.
When she heard that word
she fell right back into that old trap
of d_____ h_____,
of f_____ g_____,
of w_____ to c_____ into a m_____ h_____,
of t_____ back what she had s_____ .
She was her old self again.

2 Read out the full text.

Model text B
It was awful.
When she heard that word
she fell right back into that old trap
of disliking herself,
of feeling guilty,
of wanting to creep into a mouse-hole,
of taking back what she had said.
She was her old self again.

Text creation

1 Say that the topic 'falling back into an old trap' need not be restricted to a feeling of unworthiness.

2 As another example, present text C (by reading it out loud, displaying it for a couple of minutes, etc.).

Text C
It was terrible.
When he saw all the food in front of him
he fell right back into that old trap
of wanting all of it,
of being afraid of not getting enough,
of stuffing himself,
of eating far more than he needed.
He was his old greedy self again.

3 Present skeleton text C. The students use it to write a text.

Skeleton text C
It was _____ .
When _____
_____ fell right back into that old trap
of _____ ,
of _____ ,
of _____ ,
of _____ ,
_____ was _____ old _____ self again .

© Longman Group UK Ltd 1992

4 Publication of texts.

IT'S HIGH TIME YOU...

Preparation

Copy 20 sentences on OHP transparency (or produce a class set of handouts).

Lead-in activities

Who said this and who to?

1 Write the following sentence on the board and ask your students who might have said it and to whom. Ask them to give you words that describe the speaker's feelings.

It's high time you tidied up your room.

2 Do the same with the following additional sentences.

It's about time you learned to do this more carefully.
It's high time you learned to cook.
It's about time you got here.

Building sentences

1 Write *It's high time* and *It's about time* on the board. Give everyone about 20 seconds to look at a range of sentences like the following (on a worksheet, the board or OHP). Select your sentences with a view to your students' age.

You . . .
. . . learned to drive.
. . . did a bit of slimming.
. . . stopped making funny remarks.
. . . stopped nagging me.
. . . learned to listen.
. . . behaved yourself.
. . . cut down on alcohol.
. . . started to do some exercise.
. . . told him/her/them your opinion.
. . . sold your car.
. . . had the washing machine repaired.
. . . decorated the living room.
. . . bought some new clothes.
. . . called . . .
. . . wrote to . . .

2 Cover up the sentences (or tell your students to turn over the worksheets). Ask them to write down as many sentences as possible from memory.

3 Ask several students to read out the sentences they remember, starting each with *It's high time* or *It's about time*.

1.20

GRAMMAR
It's high time/It's about time somebody did something

LEVEL
Intermediate +

TIME
50 minutes

EXTRAS
(Optional) OHP or class set of handouts

4 Have each of your students say which sentence they dislike most and ask them to imagine the situation in which the sentence was used. Get them to try to use the same tone of voice the speaker may have used in the situation in which the sentence was originally said.

Text creation

Write the skeleton text on the board. Ask your students to write their own texts.

Skeleton text
It's high time you _____
it's high time _____ ,
it's high time _____ ,
_____ keep(s) saying.
Thanks for the advice,
but it's my time
you're talking about
and I'll decide
when to move.

If your students feel like writing their own endings (for the last 5 lines), encourage them to do so.

If you decide to ask students to read their texts out loud, spend some time guiding them in rehearsal. The first lines ought to convey the nagging, the second part ought to be spoken in a clear, firm tone.

Here are some texts from students in their fourth year.

It's high time you helped me with the housework.
It's high time you tidied up your room.
It's high time you studied harder,
Mum keeps saying.
Mum, don't be angry. It's my life.
I'll do what you want,
but, please, stop nagging.

It's high time you stopped asking this sort of question.
It's high time you started thinking about your work.
It's high time you tidied up your room
and helped with the housework,
she keeps saying.
Thank you for the advice,
but it is my problem.
You can't tell me what to do
because I hate people
who know what's best for me.

I WONDER

Presentation of model text

1 Put your students into pairs and give one partner a copy of worksheet A, the other partner worksheet B.

2 Students A and B dictate the text to each other. A starts with *When I go*, B writes it down and then dictates *for a walk* to A, and so on.

WORKSHEET A

*When I go _____ , I _____ where
_____ a book, _____ why
When I _____ , I wonder what
_____ the phone, _____ who
When I _____ growing up, _____ when.*

WORKSHEET B

*_____ for a walk, _____ wonder _____
When I read _____ , I wonder _____
_____ open a parcel, _____
When I answer _____ , I wonder _____
_____ think of _____ , I wonder _____ .*

© Longman Group UK Ltd 1992

Model text

*When I go for a walk, I wonder where
When I read a book, I wonder why
When I open a parcel, I wonder what
When I answer the phone, I wonder who
When I think of growing up, I wonder when.*

Text creation

1 Write the following prompts on the board:

		why . . .
		what . . .
When I . . . I wonder		*when . . .*
		where . . .
		who . . .

2 Ask your students to write their own texts based on the model.

1.21

GRAMMAR
*I wonder
why/when . . .*

LEVEL
Intermediate +

TIME
20-30 minutes

EXTRAS
Photocopies of worksheets A and B, one copy for each pair of learners

VARIATION

If you work with adults, you may want to use the following model text:

When I look into the mirror, I wonder who
When I'm late again, I wonder why
When I think of my holiday, I wonder where
When I dream of a pay rise, I wonder when
When I glance at the TV page, I wonder what.

ACKNOWLEDGEMENTS

The model text, *When I go for a walk* . . ., was created by Jenny Skillen during a workshop on creative grammar at Pilgrims in Canterbury.

We learnt the pair dictation technique from *Dictation* (Davis and Rinvolucri 1988, pp. 70 – 74).

CHAPTER 2

Tense, aspect and voice

HAVE YOU EVER...?

LESSON ONE

Lead-in activities

Sentences from back to back
1 Write each phrase below on one card (or sticky label). Write some phrases in one colour of pen and the rest in another.
2 Stick/pin a label/card on each student's back.
3 Ask the students to walk round silently looking at the labels on their classmates' backs. Mentally, they try to build and remember as many sentences as possible. They are *not* allowed to take notes.

Red pen
I'd like to . . .
I wouldn't like to . . .
It must be interesting to . . .
It must be fun to . . .
It must be exciting to . . .
It must be boring to . . .
It must be difficult to . . .

Blue pen
cross the Atlantic on a yacht.
go to the disco three times a week.
have more time for yourself.
climb Mount Everest.
go on a bike tour to India.
have a teacher you can talk to about everything.
have a chimpanzee as a pet.
be ten years older.
be a cook in a famous restaurant.
travel to foreign countries.
be able to talk to animals.
see a ghost.
hunt for treasure.
write for a newspaper.
be a pop star.
be a curator in a museum.

2.1

GRAMMAR
Present perfect
Have you ever . . .?

LEVEL
Lower
intermediate +

TIME
Two lessons of 40
minutes each

EXTRAS
Cards or sticky
labels; two
different coloured
pens; class set of
jumbled texts A
and B

Memory

1 Ask your learners to write down individually as many of their sentences as they can remember and to do so under two headings:

Things that are true   *Things that are not true*
for me   *for me.*

2 Divide your class into groups of about four and ask them to read their sentences out to each other. Allow time for students to talk about each others' sentences.

Telling lies and telling the truth

1 The students work in different groups of four. Tell them to write down six sentences about themselves. Each of the sentences should either start with *I'd like to . . .* or *I wouldn't like to . . ..* Some should be lies.

2 One by one the group members read out their sentences. The others listen and take notes about sentences they think are lies.

3 They then comment on what they think was true and what was a lie. This process is repeated until everybody has had their turn.

LESSON TWO

Presentation of model texts

1 Give everyone a copy of the worksheet below. Tell them to swap words between texts A and B so that the texts become meaningful. You might want to help them by underlining the parts that have been jumbled up.

WORKSHEET
Text A
Have you ever been away to an
expensive restaurant?
Have you ever dressed up awake all night?
Have you ever found to give a speech
at a friend's birthday party?
I haven't, but I think I'd like to.

Text B
Have you ever stayed as a clown?
Have you ever been invited from home?
Have you ever been asked a shooting
star in a swimming pool?
I haven't and I don't think I would like to.

© Longman Group UK Ltd 1992

2 Get one learner to read out their solution. Ask the others what they think about it. Read out the original texts.

Model text A

Have you ever been away from home?
Have you ever dressed up as a clown?
Have you ever found a shooting star in
a swimming pool?
I haven't, but I think I'd like to.

Model text B

Have you ever stayed awake all night?
Have you ever been invited to an
expensive restaurant?
Have you ever been asked to give a speech
at a friend's birthday party?
I haven't and I don't think I would like to.

Text creation

1 Ask your learners to write their own texts. In a lower level class, it might help to write the following prompts on the board:

Have you ever . . .?
Have you ever . . .?
Have you ever . . .?

I haven't, but i think I'd like to /
I haven't, and I don't think I'd like to.

VARIATION

Instead of sticking the cards on students' backs stick them on the walls. Tell your students to stand up. Give them three minutes to find as many meaningful sentences as possible. Then tell them to sit down and write these down from memory.

Here are texts written by thirteen-year-old students in their third year of English.

Have you ever met Tina Turner? *Have you ever seen a green dog?*
Have you ever travelled to New York? *Have you ever bitten the neighbour's dog?*
Have you ever interviewed a football *Have you ever been a teacher?*
star? *I haven't and I don't think I'd like to.*
I haven't, but I think I'd like to.

2.2

GRAMMAR
Present perfect continuous, *going to* future

LEVEL
Intermediate +

TIME
40 minutes

EXTRAS
Handouts of the worksheet, cut up line by line; (optional) class set of model text A

I HAVE A DREAM

Preparation

Make enough copies of the worksheet below for each student to have one line. Cut the worksheets into strips to distribute individually.

Presentation of model text

1 Ask your students to form groups of six.
2 Hand out one line of the worksheet to each student. Ask them to put the words in the strip into the correct order.
3 After the sentences are finished, the groups should use them to construct a meaningful text. Tell each group to stand in a line: the student with the first line of the text stands first, the one with the second next and so on. Then ask them to read out the words on their strips, one after the other. If there is not enough space for several groups to work simultaneously, ask two/three students to share one strip.

WORKSHEET
this/with/for/I/been/have/idea/carrying/me/years/around
it/I/been/have/of/dreaming/small/I/since/was
thought/over/I/at least/a thousand/have/it/times
think/one/and/going to/fulfil/am/day/I/I/my/dream:
own/book/little/my/to write
of/with/lots/stories/fancy/it/in.

© Longman Group UK Ltd 1992

VARIATION
In weaker groups hand out strips of words *un*jumbled.

Reconstruction of model text

1 Give everyone a copy of the model text or present it on the OHP. Get your class to memorise the text by reading it silently to themselves line by line.

Model text
I have been carrying this idea around with me for years
I have been dreaming of it since I was small.
I have thought it over at least a thousand times
and one day I think I am going to fulfil my dream:
to write my own little book
with lots of fancy stories in it.

© Longman Group UK Ltd 1992

2 Ask everyone to cover their text and reconstruct it in writing with the help of the following prompts:

I have been . . .
I have been . . .
since/for . . . ,
and one day . . .:

3 Ask the students to compare what they have written with the original text.

Text creation

1 Tell the class about a dream of yours. Ask everyone to work in pairs and to take it in turns to tell each other about a dream they have had for years.

2 Ask everyone to write their own texts about their dream(s) based on the structure of the model text. In addition to the prompts above, you could offer the following:

I have been waiting to/for . . .
I have been dreaming of . . .
I have been wanting to . . .
I have been hoping to . . .
I have been thinking to . . .

Here is a student text:

I have been thinking about this problem for years.
I have been feeling this since my thirteenth birthday.
I have tried to bury it deep inside a thousand times
and on the first lovely day in spring
I think I am going to tell it to the others.
What?
That's my secret.

FROM A PROBLEM PAGE

Lead-in activities

Listening

1 Briefly explain/elicit what problem pages and agony aunts are. If anyone has never read a problem page, read an example out to them. Here is one from *Truth is Stranger . . .* (Landers 1968, pp.76-77). Read text A slowly and make eye contact whenever you pause. Explain any words your students do not seem to understand.

Text A
Dear Ann Landers
My dad used to have a great build in his younger days. But a lot of beer has gone down the hatch since then and now he's sort of fat. Dad insists on

2.3

GRAMMAR
Present tense for narration

LEVEL
Intermediate +

TIME
30 – 40 minutes

EXTRAS
(Optional) class set of jumbled text C

sitting around the house in swimming trunks. When my friends come over I'm embarrassed. My mother doesn't like it either. Every now and then she'll say, 'Harold, go put on a robe.' But he pays no attention. My dad is wonderful and I love all 220 pounds of him, but do you think he should sit in the living room in swimming trunks when I have company?
Ghandi's daughter

Dear Daughter
When your mother gives out with 'Harold, go put on a robe,' Harold should go put on a robe. You wouldn't sit in the living room in your bathing suit when Dad entertains business friends, would you? Point this out to him. It might help.

2 Tell your students that you are going to read out another agony letter but that it was not written by a person but by a thing. Read out text B, leaving out the line *I am a lamp-post.*

3 Ask them to guess what the thing is. If necessary, write questions for the guessing game on the board. For example :

Is it made of . . .?
Can we see it in the classroom?
Have people got it in their houses?

4 When someone has guessed that it's a lamp-post, ask the class to guess why the lamp-post is writing a letter.

Text B
From a problem page

Dear Maureen,
I am a lamp-post.
Every Saturday evening at five o'clock
three boys
wearing blue and white scarves
blue and white hats
waving their arms in the air
and shouting,
come my way.
Sometimes they kick me.
Sometimes they kiss me.
What should I do
to get them to make up their minds?
Yours bewilderedly,
Annie Onlight.

Michael Rosen, *Wouldn't You Like to Know*, Puffin Books 1987 p.75

Presentation of model text

Present a jumbled version of text C on a worksheet or OHP. Ask
students to number the lines in the correct order.

Jumbled text C
a tiny, old man and his big dog
What should I do?
when you enter the park.
and while the man looks away
Dear Maureen,
Yours miserably
come to the park
I'm an oak tree
the dog . . .
Douglas Trim
the first on the right
Every day at about six o'clock
well, I'm sure you can imagine.

© Longman Group UK Ltd 1992

Model text C (key)
6   *a tiny, old man and his big dog*
11   *What should I do?*
4   *when you enter the park.*
8   *and while the man looks away*
1   *Dear Maureen,*
12   *Yours miserably*
7   *come to the park*
2   *I'm an oak tree*
9   *the dog . . .*
13   *Douglas Trim*
3   *the first on the right*
5   *Every day at about six o'clock*
10   *well, I'm sure you can imagine.*

Text creation

Ask your students to write, individually or in pairs, their own texts
based on the model.

2.4

GRAMMAR
Present perfect
(completion),
quantifying nouns

LEVEL
Lower
intermediate +

TIME
30 – 40 minutes

EXTRAS
Bottle (optional)

COSMIC COCKTAIL

Lead-in activities

The teacher's favourite cocktail

1 Bring along to your class a bottle containing a brightly coloured liquid, or draw a bottle on the board with different coloured stars in it (see figure 4). Say that this is your favourite drink and that you got the recipe for it from a magician many years ago. Tell your students what the drink is called. Invent a fancy name, such as *Cosmic Cocktail*.

Fig. 4

2 Before going further, decide on the ingredients. Do not tell your class what they are. Ask them to guess the ingredients. In order to make the guessing easier write the first letter of each ingredient on the board like this (but without the answers).

a bit of the	*m _ _ _ _ w _ _*	*(milky way)*
a bit of a	*c _ _ _ _*	*(comet)*
bits of	*s _ _ _ _*	*(stars)*
three	*g _ _ _ _ _ _ _*	*(galaxies)*
some drops of	*s _ _ _ w _ _ _ _*	*(salt water)*
a spoonful of	*h _ _ _ _*	*(honey)*

Answer questions with *Yes* or *No* only.

Presentation and reconstruction of model text

1 Write the following model text on the board.

Model text
I have blended everything nicely:
a bit of the milky way,
a comet
several stars
and three galaxies.
I have added salt water
and honey

(I like it sweet you know).
I have boiled it
for half an hour
and stirred it carefully.
Maybe you would like to taste it:
my wonderful cosmic cocktail.

2 Give the class 30 seconds to study the text.
3 Then rub out everything except for the following:

I have _____ :
a bit of _____ ,
a _____
several _____
and three _____ .
I have _____
and _____
(I _____)
I have _____
for _____
and _____ .
Maybe _____ :
my wonderful _____ .

4 Students try to write the full text in pairs. Read out the original once more and ask them to correct their versions of the text. Leave the prompts on the board. Your students might need them in the writing stage later on.

Collecting language
1 Revise or teach the following verbs and noun phrases, so that your students will have a greater variety of language at their disposal in the writing stage. Write them on the board.

Verbs
to mix / to blend / to boil / to grind / to cut /
to add / to stir / to put in

Quantities
a litre of / a pint of / a kilogramme of /
a pound of / a packet of / a tin of / a bottle of /
a cup of / a glass of / a piece of /
a spoonful of / a bit of / pieces of / some drops of

2 Give your class time to study the words on the board.
3 Revise the words by forming them without making a sound. The students have to guess the words from the movements of your lips.
4 Cover the words up and ask the students to remember as many as they can.

Text creation

Ask your students to create their own texts based on the model. Mention that if anyone decides to use time markers like *first, second, then,* they will have to shift to the past tense.

Here is a text written by a student in the second year of English.

We have blended some western things:
pieces of cowboys
an old hat
and a gun.
We have added a cactus
and some sand.
We've ground some lassos
and saddles and stirred everything
carefully.
Maybe you would like to taste it:
our wonderful western cocktail.

2.5

GRAMMAR
Past passive

LEVEL
Intermediate +

TIME
40–50 minutes

EXTRAS
(Optional) OHP or two large sheets of poster paper; pen or stick

WHAT A DAY!

Preparation

Copy the picture puzzle and skeleton text onto (separate) OHP transparencies or large sheets of poster paper.

Presentation of model text

1 Display the picture puzzle (figure 5).

Fig. 5

2 Remain silent for one or two minutes. Try to elicit words from the students. If someone guesses a word correctly, point to the corresponding picture/letter(s) in the puzzle and nod your head.

3 Point to the first line of the picture puzzle. Elicit the first line of the model text below and write it on the board. Proceed like this with all the other lines of the model text.

Model text

My biology teacher was bitten by a cat
My brother was kissed by a vampire
My dog was kidnapped by an eagle
My boyfriend was run over by a tricycle
My hamster was eaten by a snake
and I was seen by my mother
as I was pouring a bowl
of tomato soup
out of the kitchen window.
What a day!

First text reconstruction

1 Tell the students to rehearse the model text by reading it half out loud to themselves.
2 Form pairs. Remove the model text/switch off the OHP.
3 Ask the pairs to look at the picture puzzle and write the model text.
4 Re-form the class. Ask someone to come to the board.
5 Get the other students to dictate the text to the person at the board. Do not interfere, even if the text on the board is different from the original.
6 Form pairs again.
7 Display the skeleton text. Ask the pairs to check their texts against the text on the board and the skeleton text. Tell them to add to their texts and correct them. Do not interfere as long as your students do not get stuck. Allow about three minutes.
8 Display the full model text again. Get students to check and correct their version against it.

Skeleton text

M _ b _ _ _ _ _ _   t _ _ _ _ _ _   w _ _ b _ _ _ _ _   b _ a c _ _
M _ b _ _ _ _ _ _   w _ _ k _ _ _ _ _   b _ a v _ _ _ _ _ _
M _ d _ _ w _ _ k _ _ _ _ _ _ _ _   b _ a _ e _ _ _ _
M _ b _ _ _ _ _ _ _   w _ _ r _ _ o _ _ _ b _ a t _ _ _ _ _ _ _
M _ h _ _ _ _ _ _   w _ _ e _ _ _ _   b _ a s _ _ _ _
a _ _ l w _ _ s _ _ _ b _ m _ m _ _ _ _ _
a _ l w _ _ p _ _ _ _ _ _ ab _ _ _
o _ t _ _ _ _ _ s _ _ _
o _ _ o _ t _ _ k _ _ _ _ _ _ w _ _ _ _ _ .
W _ _ _ a d _ _ !

Second text reconstruction

1 Ask your class to put their texts face down on their desks. Continue to display the skeleton text.
2 Lead a choral reconstruction of the text. Guide by moving a pen or stick at reading speed through the text.

Third text reconstruction

1 Now switch off the OHP/remove the text skeleton.
2 Lead another choral reconstruction of the text.

Text creation

Everyone writes their own texts. Allow about ten minutes.
The following text is by a thirteen-year-old in the third year of English.

My mother was bitten by a dog
My sister was bitten by a snake
My brother was thrown into a swimming pool
I was knocked down by a car
when I was crossing the street
My cousin was kissed by a budgie
and my boyfriend fell ill
when a pumpkin was dropped on his head.
What a day!

EXTENSION
When you have corrected the students' texts, ask them to write a skeleton version of their text as homework. These student skeleton texts can then be redistributed and used for further practice.

VARIATION
If you work with adults, you may want to use the following text:

At the office
a door was slammed in my face
I was told several lies
and my new computer programme
was eaten by a virus.
In the pub
I was looked up and down
by all the men
and when I blew my top
I was politely asked to leave.
When I came home,
I found out that my phone had been disconnected
and there was no way
of sharing my anger
with anybody.

I'M GOING TO . . .

Preparation

Write several commands on flash cards, for example *Put on your hat*, *Blow out the candle*, etc.

Lead-in activities

You can do it
1 Get the students to stand in a circle.
2 Give a command such as: *Read a newspaper*, *Clean your teeth*, accompanying it with mime. Encourage everyone to imitate you. They need not speak. Choose your commands according to language and situations you have taught so far.
3 Change to giving the commands without mime and gesture.
4 Elicit the commands from the students by miming the action.
5 Ask your students to stand in two rows like this:

```
    S   S
    S   S
    S   S
    S   S
    S   S
      T
```

6 Say that you have commands written on flash cards. Tell the first student in each row to mime the action that they see on the flash card you show and then go to the last position in the group. Do several examples and then have a competition between teams. The first of the two front students to correctly mime a flash card command scores a point. Both go to the back of their line. Flash a new card for the two new students at the front.

What am I going to do?
1 Write *You are going to* . . . on the board.
2 Elicit sentences such as *You are going to have a cup of tea*, *You are going to post a letter*, *You are going to go to bed*. Mime what a person usually does just *before* the action you want to elicit from the students. For example, putting a tea bag into a mug and pouring hot water on it (before having a cup of tea).
3 When they are familiar with the idea, ask students to come out and do some miming in front of the class. The other learners guess what the student who is miming *is going to do*.

VARIATION
1 Display a list of sentences on poster paper or OHP (see the sample sentences).

2.6

GRAMMAR
Going to, past tense

LEVEL
Elementary – lower intermediate

TIME
50 minutes

EXTRAS
Flash cards (optional), a list of sentences on poster paper or OHP transparency

2 Give your students twenty seconds or so to remember as many sentences as possible.

3 Elicit the sentences from the class by miming a prior action for each.

You are going to drive a car.
You are going to clean your teeth.
You are going to drink a cup of tea.
You are going to play a guitar.
You are going to pick a flower.
You are going to listen to a record.
You are going to paint a picture.
You are going to ride a motorbike.
You are going to pick some apples.
You are going to ride a horse.
You are going to watch TV.
You are going to go for a walk in the rain.

Broken promises

1 Tell the class about one or two situations in which you had intended to do something but never did. For example:

You know, last Sunday I said to myself, 'I'm going to write this letter to Bill.'
You know what happened? The telephone rang and a friend asked me to come over to his place. So I went and didn't write the letter.

2 Ask everyone to think of similar situations and talk about these in small groups.

Presentation of model text

1 Read out the model text (below) twice.

2 Ask everyone to close their eyes and imagine what the place the person lives in looks like. Read the text out again.

3 Ask several students what they have visualised. For example: Is the room big? Are there any curtains? Make sure they understand that the *I'm going to* . . . sentences were said either in the morning or at the beginning of the afternoon.

Model text for young learners
'I'm going to tidy up my room
I'm going to write a letter
I'm going to help Mum
I'm going to do my homework,'
I said to myself
but then
I watched TV all afternoon.

Text creation

1 Now write the following prompts on the board and tell your students to write their own texts. Allow about five minutes.

'I'm going to _____
I'm going to _____
I'm going to _____
I'm going to _____
I said to myself
but then

_____

2 As students finish, they pair up or form groups and read each other their texts. If some people finish their writing much sooner than others, they can keep finding new partners.

VARIATION

If you work with adults you may want to use the following model text:

'I'm going to eat less
I'm going to cut down on smoking
I'm going to do more exercise
I'm going to drink less coffee,'
I said to myself
but by Friday the week had turned out
just the same as all the others.

THAT'S COOL

Lead-in activities

Building vocabulary

1 Tell your students that you'll show some words or word gaps for only a couple of seconds. Ask them to remember as many as possible and to note them on a sheet of paper.

2 Show words from the model text (on an OHP or a poster). When we tried out the activity with fourteen-year-olds, we used the following words:

people build mountain shout feel
spend more money on kill fast in a row
cool bombs bored then world

3 After removing the word list elicit the words. Write them on the board *exactly* as students give them.

4 Display the words again. Students check the words on the board against the list on the OHP/poster paper. Explain any words they do not understand.

5 Ask them to form meaningful sentences with the words.

2.7

GRAMMAR
When + present

LEVEL
Intermediate +

TIME
50 minutes

EXTRAS
Class set of the worksheet; three strips of paper for each student

Presentation of model text

1 Add *watching*, *children*, *than*, *kill* to the list above.
2 Hand out copies of the worksheet.

WORKSHEET
When it is _____
to get _____ *by* _____
six programmes _____ ,
when it is cool
to _____ *cars*
_____ *on* _____ ,
when it is cool
to _____ *yourself on a* _____ *motorbike,*
when it is cool
to _____ _____
that can _____ *the* _____ *of the* _____ ,
_____ *I* _____ *like standing*
on the highest _____
in the world and
_____*ing 'No'.*

© Longman Group UK Ltd 1992

3 Ask various students to read out their solutions. Then read out the full text:

Model text
When it is cool
to get bored by watching
six programmes in a row,
when it is cool
to spend more money on cars
than on children,
when it is cool
to kill yourself on a fast motorbike,
when it is cool
to build bombs
that can kill the people of the world,
then I feel like standing
on the highest mountain
in the world and
shouting 'No'.

Text creation

1 Ask your students to work in groups of four to six. Each student writes at least three sentences beginning with *When it's cool* on a different strip of paper.
2 Collect the strips of paper and pass them on to another group so

that each group has at least twelve strips from another group. They read through them, select those which form a meaningful text and add an ending that starts with *then I feel like . . . .*

3 Each group chooses a spokesperson who reads out their text.

SURPRISE, SURPRISE

Preparation

Copy the model text (page 77) onto an OHP transparency or copy it onto index cards, one word per card.

LESSON ONE

Lead-in activities

Circle clap

1 Get your class to sit in a circle.

2 Clap your hands once. The student sitting on your right has to clap hands immediately after you. Then it's the second student's turn and so on. Practise for a while in one direction until you get a smooth, rhythmical clap going round fast, then change direction.

Associated words

1 Announce that you are going to say a word, and that instead of clapping, everyone, in turn, says a word that they associate with the word mentioned by the person before them.

2 Get your learners to do this as quickly and as rhythmically as possible. For example:

wood – squirrel – high tree – wind – ocean – across . . .

Disassociated words

Proceed as above, but this time everyone says a word they think has nothing to do with the word before. For example:

wood – salt – good – coat – really – dictionary . . .

Impromptu story: associated words

Say that you are going to tell a story. Add that anyone can interrupt you by shouting out a word which you haven't used yet but which the story brings to mind in some way. You then have to fit that word into the story. For example:

Teacher: Once upon a time there was
Student 1: King

GRAMMAR
Past simple and progressive

LEVEL
Intermediate +

TIME
2 lessons of 40 – 50 minutes each

EXTRAS
Model text copied on OHP transparency or 44 – 45 index cards

Teacher: Yes, a king. He had a beautiful garden
Student 2: Witch
Teacher: The king had a beautiful garden that he really enjoyed, but there was one problem. At the back of the garden there was a little hut and in this hut lived a witch.
Student 3: Midnight

Impromptu story: disassociated words
Proceed as above, but this time there will be more surprise elements because the students must shout out words which they think have nothing to do with the story told so far. For example:

Teacher: Once upon a time there was
Student 1: Steam engine
Teacher: An old steam engine.
Student 2: Cow
Teacher: You will probably find it hard to believe, but this steam engine fell in love with a cow. One day
Student 3: Hot dog
Teacher: Hot dog? Yes, one day the steam engine wanted to treat the cow to lunch. The cow liked hot dogs. So they both went to a fast food restaurant.
Student 4: Knife
Teacher: Knife, well, the cow had brought her own knife because . . .

Presentation of model text

1 Place your transparency on the OHP with everything hidden but the first word.
2 Elicit the text word by word, each time asking students to guess the next hidden word. Use two sheets of paper to slowly reveal the text word by word: move one sheet of paper horizontally, the other one down, line by line, as shown in figure 6.

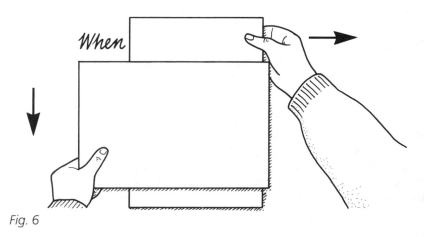

Fig. 6

Give as little verbal help as possible, but use as many of the following types of prompt as you want:

a mime, gesture
b reveal the first letter of the next hidden word
c reveal words letter by letter
d confirm or deny the word in grammatical terms (e.g. 'No, plural', 'Use a different tense', 'Right, it is a verb').

Model text
When I got home last night
I found a toad on my bed.
It was snoring.
I was so frightened
I ran to the front door.
When I got there
It was sitting on the doorstep grinning,
'My name's John,' it said
and disappeared.   © Longman Group UK Ltd 1992

VARIATION
If you do not have access to an OHP, try this:
1 Write words on cards, one word or word group per card.
2 Elicit the text bit by bit as above. Display the cards either by sticking them on the board with sellotape (or Blu-Tack) or by arranging them on the floor with you all sitting around them in a circle.

LESSON TWO

Text reconstruction

1 Cover up some words in the text (or remove some of the cards).
2 Elicit the missing words.
3 Repeat this several times, each time deleting more words.

Text creation

1 Write the following prompts on the board:

When I (the old man/my sister/friend etc.)___
I (he/she etc.) found/realised/met/___
___ was/were___
I (he/she)___
I (he/she)___
When___
___ was/were___
___
___

2 The students write their own texts, with the help of the prompts.

Text sharing

Get the class into a big circle. Ask everybody, one by one, to read their text out loud.

ACKNOWLEDGEMENTS
We learnt the hand-clapping activity and the impromptu story-telling techniques from Norman Skillen. The model text is based on a text handed in to us during a workshop at Pilgrims. It is signed 'Shirley'.

2.9

GRAMMAR
Might

LEVEL
Intermediate +

TIME
60 – 80 minutes

EXTRAS
None

WORRIED

Lead-in activities

A story
Tell your group a story (such as the story of the boy and the coin below) in which an object gives somebody strength or exercises some curative power. Do not read out the story or tell it from notes. Add details if you want to make it as lively as possible.

On his way to school, Tom had to pass a garden with a fence. Behind it there was always a big dog. Tom was worried that the dog might come out in the street one day. When one day it really did, Tom quickly crossed the street to avoid the dog and went into a shop. The old shopkeeper realised that the boy was afraid and gave him a coin. He said it would help him. When the boy left the shop, there was the dog outside. Tom put his hand in his pocket. He held the coin firmly and his fear passed. The next day he even dared to stroke the dog when it was out in the street again.

Power objects
Elicit words for things that might have curative powers. Also elicit some information about these things, for example:

Student 1:   *Picture postcard.*
Teacher: *What's the story behind it?*
Student 1:   *My girlfriend sent it to me and it makes me feel good when I look at it.*
Student 2:   *Fluffy animal. I always have my fluffy hamster with me when I have a test.*

As you elicit words, write them on the board.

Changes

1 Write the following pairs of words on the board too:

afraid	*courageous*
worried	*calm*
depressed	*full of energy*
shy	*outgoing*
sullen	*lively*

2 Explain the words, giving at least one situation to clarify the meaning.

3 Ask your students to move so that there is some open space in the classroom.

4 Tell them that they are going to do an exercise in which they have to remember situations from the past, but that there won't be any talking.

5 Ask everybody to find a bit of free space to stand in.

6 Tell them to think of situations in their past which fit each one of the pairs of words on the board. Give examples:

Situation one

Some years ago I stayed in a lonely motel in Arizona. During the night I heard a couple of shots being fired. I tried to peer out into the dark night, but couldn't see anything. I couldn't get any sleep because I felt terribly afraid.

Situation two

Some months ago I was walking home from a restaurant late at night. When I turned the corner I came upon a group of youngsters who seemed to be having an argument with an elderly man. My first reaction was to turn back, but when I realised there was something threatening about the situation, I walked straight up towards them. I was surprised how courageous I felt. The gang disappeared and the man told me how glad he was that I had turned up.

7 Allow enough time for them to think and recall. Ask them to stand in one space on the floor for the 'negative' situation and in another one for the 'positive' one.

8 Tell them literally to step into the space for the 'negative' situation and to go through it again in their mind. Give them enough time for this procedure.

9 Ask them to step out of the 'negative' situation and literally step into the 'positive' one by stepping into their positive space on the floor. Allow enough time for them to remember the situation again. Remind them to pay attention to any memories of colours, sounds, tastes and body movement.

10 Ask them all to choose one or more of the 'talismans' or 'power objects' listed on the board – ones which would fit into their 'positive' recollection. Allow time for this again.

11 Ask everyone literally to step back into the 'negative' situation again (by stepping into the corresponding floor space). But this time they should imagine taking along their chosen power object(s) and the memories of the colours, sounds and tastes from the positive situation. Ask them to reflect how their perception of the 'negative' situation changes.

It might be helpful if you list the above steps on the board.

Sharing

If you have the feeling that your students want to share their experience, ask them to do so in pairs. Do tell them, however, that sharing means *listening*, but *not* judging or commenting in any way.

Presentation of model text

Read out the model text twice. Before reading the second time, ask everyone to imagine what the person looks like.

Model text

I was worried that I might lose my purse
I was worried that I might miss the bus
I was worried that I might forget to tell him
I was worried that he might not get any tickets
I was worried that he might not catch the train
and I was worried that he might not find me.
'Please, no more worries,' I said to myself.
And I think I've learned the trick.
When I get worried, I pick up
a magic thing and say,
'No more worries, I've had enough.'

Text creation

1 Write the following skeleton text on the board. Everyone writes a text according to the model.
2 Publication of texts.

Skeleton text

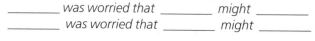

_____ *was worried that* _____ *might* _____
_____ *was worried that* _____ *might* _____

_____
_____

VARIATION

If you work with adults you may want to use the following model text:

He was worried
that he might not be dressed properly.
He was worried
that he might be considered stupid
when putting forward his ideas.
He was worried
that he might have laughed too much.
And he was worried
that he might have taken up
too much of his friends' time.
But on the day when he found out
that life was not a rehearsal
he packed all his worries into a bag,
walked on to a bridge
and flung them into the river.

ACKNOWLEDGEMENT
We learnt the technique for the 'changes' activity from Robert Dilts.

I'M AHEAD OF MY TIME

Preparation

Write the model text on transparency or on the strips of stiff paper, one line per strip.

Lead-in activities

Mime daily routines
1 Mime various actions (having a cup of tea, reading a paper, driving a car) and ask the learners to guess what you are doing.
2 Write the words on the board or ask a student to do so. Make sure everyone gets the meaning and pronunciation of the words right.

You like, dislike, don't mind
1 Draw three columns on the board and draw a face on top of each (see figure 7 overleaf). Tell your students that the three faces stand for *I like, I don't like* and *I don't mind.*
2 Write the first letters of various daily routines in the columns and ask students to guess what you like, dislike or don't mind doing.
3 Encourage your learners to ask questions concerning each activity, for example:

2.10

GRAMMAR
While + past progressive

LEVEL
Lower intermediate +

TIME
40–50 minutes

EXTRAS
OHP transparency or 14 strips of stiff paper

Student 1: I think you don't like getting up.
Teacher: That's right.
Student 2: You don't like to shave.
Teacher: That's also true. I don't like shaving.
Student 3: Why don't you like it?
*Teacher: Well, sometimes I cut myself, it takes time, I have to do it
                    again the next morning.*

Fig. 7

Guessing game
1 Form pairs.
2 Each student writes down two activities they think their partner
   likes / dislikes / doesn't mind doing.
3 They read out their speculations and their partners confirm or deny
   them. Ideally, students should work with partners they do not know
   well. Time permitting, they may change partners several times.

Mental images
1 Tell your students that you are going to say a stem sentence which
   you want them to finish in writing.
2 Give an example: *While I was coming to school . . .* Let's say you were
   thinking about the homework you didn't do, so you write down *I was
   thinking about the homework I didn't do.*
     When you have said a stem sentence, ask everyone to close their
   eyes and to wait for a clear mental image of what they had been
   doing. Only when they have this image do they complete the stem.
   For example:

Teacher: While I was washing up I was thinking of . . .
Student 1: A large garden.
Student 2: A letter I wanted to write.

Presentation of model text

1 Show your students the first line of the model text very briefly (OHP
   or flash cards). Tell them to write it down. Use the same technique
   with each line.

2 Ask everyone to compare their text with a partner.
3 Ask several students, one by one, to read out their texts.
4 Display the whole text. Read it out as well, in order to give your students a model of pronunciation and intonation.

Model text
While I was having breakfast
I was thinking about my boss.
While I was crawling along in heavy traffic
I was thinking about the pile of work
waiting for me.
While I was at work
I was thinking about a peaceful evening
in front of the TV,
and while I was watching TV
I was thinking about how difficult it is
to fall asleep.
I am always
ahead of my time.

Text creation

Write the skeleton text on the board. Ask your students to write their own texts. They may change the last two sentences if they want.

Skeleton text
While I(he/she)was _____

_____

while _____

_____

while _____

_____

and while _____

_____

I am (he/she is)
always ahead of my (his/her) time.

2.11

GRAMMAR
Third person -s,
doesn't

LEVEL
Elementary

TIME
30 minutes

EXTRAS
(Optional) OHP

Preparation

If you have an OHP, write the model text on a transparency.

Presentation of model text

1 Present the text below on an OHP transparency or on the board.
2 Read the text out.
3 Tell your students to close their eyes. Ask them to imagine what the girl looks like. Read the text a second time.
4 Ask them a couple of questions about her looks.

> Model text
> *She likes animals*
> *she likes flowers*
> *she likes good stories*
> *but*
> *she doesn't like*
> *one thing:*
> *lies.*

Text reconstruction

1 Put a mask on the transparency (or erase words from the board) so that your students can only see the following:

> *She* _____
> *she* _____
> *she* _____
> *but*
> *she* _____
>
> _____
> _____

2 Ask them to say the original version.

Text creation

1 Tell your learners to close their eyes and think of a person they want to write about.
2 Ask them to create their own texts based on the above prompts. Have your students read their texts out loud. They may, of course, use *he* instead of *she*.

Here are two texts written by ten-year-old beginners.

She likes English	*She likes beautiful flowers*
she likes French	*she likes her dolls*
she likes biology	*she likes boys*

but
she doesn't like
one thing:
unfair teachers.

but
she doesn't like
two things:
thieves and school.

INCIDENTS

2.12

GRAMMAR
Past tense for
narrative,
questions about
the past

LEVEL
Lower
intermediate +

TIME
40 – 50 minutes

EXTRAS
A class set of the
model text

Presentation of model text

1 Form groups of three or four.
2 Assign a letter (A, B, C, D) to each student.
3 Give everyone a copy of the model text.
4 Ask them to read the text and make up a background story for it.
   You may want to give them a few guiding questions for their work.

Model text
This morning I saw a woman
on the bus to school.
Her face was swollen
and her eyes were filled with tears.
Did she notice that everybody was
staring at her?
Did she see the two kids
laughing at her behind her back?
Did she hope that somebody would
ask her about her sorrow or
did she want to be left alone?
I did not try to talk to her either.
Do not ask me why.

Guiding questions
What do you think had happened to the woman before she got on the
bus?
How many people were involved in the incident?
How did each of these behave?
What do you think was the motive for their behaviour?
What do you think happened after the woman got off the bus?

© Longman Group UK Ltd 1992

Story-telling
1 Form four new groups by putting all the As, Bs, Cs and Ds together.
2 Ask everyone to tell the other group members their version.

Finding a similar situation
1 The narrator of the incident described above was not quite sure of
   what was going on. Ask your students to identify with the narrator
   and speculate about his or her feelings in the situation. Ask them if

they would have reacted likewise or totally differently.

2 Allow several minutes for everyone to recall a situation where they had feelings similar to those of the narrator.

3 Ask them to express in the form of a mind map what they remember about this situation. Figure 8 shows a student's mind map.

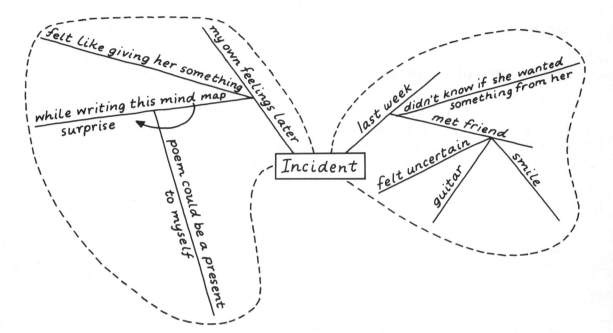

Fig. 8

Text creation

1 Point out or elicit the following about the model text:

a opening statement (lines 1 and 2) – general

b focus on person (lines 3 – 4) – specific

c four reflective questions (lines 5 – 11)

d narrator's behaviour (line 12)

e addressing the reader (line 13)

2 Ask your students to write their own texts based on this non-linguistic structure.

This example is by the student who produced the mind map above.

Last week I met a friend of mine,
a guitar in her hand ,
her eyes a little sad ,
her lips trying to smile,
her hand reaching out for something.
Did she notice I was there?

Did she want me to talk to her?
Did she really want me to do something
for her?
I wrote a poem for her.
I could have written it to myself.

Elisabeth Schweiger

RIDING A CROCODILE

Preparation

(Optional) write infinitives of irregular verbs on flash cards, one per card.

Lead-in activity

Back writing
1 Tell your class to get together in threes.
2 Ask the As in each group to look at you, the Bs and Cs to turn their backs to you. Nobody is allowed to talk. Mime an action (one expressable by an irregular verb) or show it on a flash card. The As now turn around and write the past form of this verb on the Bs' backs with their fingers. The Bs write the past participle of the verb on the Cs' backs. The Cs, in turn, note down the infinitive of the verb on a piece of paper and put it face down on a desk. Demonstrate the activity first with three students in front of the class. Then continue with ten to twenty words.
3 Read out the list of verbs you started with and ask each group to check how many of the verbs they got right.

Presentation of model text

1 Present the skeleton text and ask your learners to complete it in pairs (each dash stands for one letter):

Skeleton text
Ha _ _ yo _ ev _ _ , ev _ _ , ev _ _
i _ yo _ _ li _ _
ri _ _ _ _ a cr _ _ _ _ _ _ _ ?
N _ , I ha _ _ ne _ _ _ , ne _ _ _ , ne _ _ _
ri _ _ _ _ a cr _ _ _ _ _ _ _ ,
b _ _ I on _ _
ro _ _ a dr _ _ _ _ .

2 Ask a few learners, one by one, to read out their texts. Then read out the original:

2.13

GRAMMAR
Present perfect
(*Have you
ever . . . ?*)

LEVEL
Lower
intermediate

TIME
20 – 30 minutes

EXTRAS
(Optional) flash
cards; OHP
necessary for the
variation

Model text
Have you ever, ever, ever
in your life
ridden a crocodile?
No, I have never, never, never
ridden a crocodile,
but I once
rode a dragon.

Text creation

Students write their own texts based on the model.
The following texts were written by twelve-year-olds in their second
year of English.

Have you ever, ever, ever   *Have you ever, ever,ever*
in your life   *in your life*
swum in tomato soup?   *shouted at your teacher?*
No, I have never, never, never   *No, I have never, never, never*
swum in tomato soup,   *shouted at my teacher,*
but I once   *but she once*
found a fly in my tomato soup.   *shouted at me.*

VARIATION

1 Show a range of irregular verbs on flashcards and tell your learners
   to mime the verbs.
2 Now using the same cards, elicit the past form of each verb and ask
   the students to say sentences using the past starting with *Once . . ..*
   Proceed like this for a few minutes to give your learners sufficient
   practice of the structure before you go on to the next stage.
3 Display the following 12 sentences on the OHP, read them out and
   clarify the meaning of words your learners don't know.

   Have you ever eaten an earthworm?
   Have you ever written a love poem?
   Have you ever lost your schoolbag?
   Have you ever drunk cod-liver oil?
   Have you ever told a lie?
   Have you ever found some money?
   Have you ever caught a bat?
   Have you ever seen a ghost?
   Have you ever broken a window?
   Have you ever bought some junk?
   Have you ever ridden a camel?
   Have you ever been to London?

4 Students study the list for a minute and then you switch off the OHP.
5 Ask them each to say the sentence they like best.

6 Present the model text on page 88, then ask your students to write their own texts.

If you work with adults you may want to use the following model text:

Have you ever, ever, ever
in your life
made another person look like a perfect idiot?
No, I've never, never, never
made another person look like a perfect idiot,
but I once
made a complete fool of myself.

I LIKE PEOPLE WHO . . .

Preparation

Before class, ask students to bring along a photo of themselves.

Lead-in activities

Opening up a field of awareness
1 Show your class a photo of someone you like.
2 Tell them a few things about this person, for example, how you got to know him/her, a story about him/her, etc.
3 Ask your students to work in groups and write a list of this person's positive qualities. They should include positive qualities that *they* think this person has, not only the things you have told them about.
4 Ask your students what they have written and list what they say on the board, for example:

He/She	*likes to laugh.*
	helps you when you have a problem.
	cares about doing things right.
	hardly ever gets angry.

5 Ask the students to think of people they like, and ask them to add positive qualities to the list you have started.

I like you because
1 Arrange your class in a circle sitting down.
2 Throw your ball of string to one student and tell this person what you like about them. For example, 'Peter, I like you because you are a good listener.'
3 Ask Peter to wind the string around his finger and throw the ball to another person in the group addressing them in the same way (e.g. 'Karen, I like you because you are friendly.')

2.14

GRAMMAR
Present simple, affirmation and negation (*I like / I don't like*), defining relative clause

LEVEL
Lower intermediate +

TIME
At least 80 – 100 minutes (or a series of 2 or 3 45-minute lessons)

EXTRAS
A ball of string or wool; photos; one large sheet of poster paper for each student; cassette of soft, meditative music

4 Allow seven to ten minutes for the game. Then go back to the list you have started and, with the help of your students, add a few more positive qualities.

NOTE

The preceding activity can noticably enhance positive feelings that already exist among participants. Less obvious, perhaps, is the potential of an activity like this for alerting you to any participants who are isolated from the rest of the class. A teacher experienced in facilitating group dynamics can use the insights gained to integrate the student(s) into the group. (See especially Stanford 1977; also Davis and Rinvolucri 1990.)

Positive self presentation

1 Ask your students to think of qualities other people like about them. Tell them that various people like different things about each of us. What their parents like about them might be totally different from what their best friend at school or their favourite teacher likes. Perhaps add a few examples about yourself.

2 Ask your students to stick their photographs in the middle of a big sheet of poster paper and to write around the photo the positive qualities they think others see in them.

3 When they have finished, get them to close their eyes and imagine themselves five years on from now.

4 Play some soft, meditative music. You can help your students with the visualisation of their positive future self by guiding them, as follows.

Find a comfortable sitting position . . . with your back straight and your feet firmly on the ground . . . and for a while focus on the contact you have with your chair . . . and the floor below you . . . and while you are listening to the sound of the music . . . and the sound of my voice . . . you can also direct your attention to other noises you can hear at the moment . . . the noise of the cars passing by . . . and the footsteps of the people walking along the corridor past our classroom (substitute whatever sounds you can really hear in your class for these) . . . and now you can listen to your own breath . . . as you breathe in and breathe out . . . in a natural rhythm . . . in and out . . . and while you are sitting there in your chair . . . listening to my words . . . imagine yourself five years on from now . . . imagine that you are actually travelling into the year X . . . on a day like today . . . you are now five years older . . . you can feel that you have grown . . . and developed in a very positive way . . . you have made things possible for yourself that you were dreaming would come true five years ago . . . just feel what it is like to have all these positive qualities that you now have . . . and how other people react to you as you have changed . . . and how you enjoy this . . . take some time now to experience this new feeling . . . while you're listening to the sound of the music (allow two minutes) . . . you feel very light and happy and now you slowly start walking back through the years to the here and now. Take your time, all the time you need and slowly,

slowly come back to the here and now. Slowly open your eyes and stretch a little, welcome back to your classroom.

5 Ask your students to add their 'future' positive qualities to their posters. Tell them to use the same language structure as above so that they actually present themselves as having these qualities already.

Presentation of model text

1 Write the first two words of the model text on the board.
2 Elicit the text from the learners word by word, giving them as little verbal help as possible.
3 As you elicit the text, write it in the vertical layout shown below. (If you do not have freckles, you might want to adapt the text slightly so that it fits you personally.)

Model text
I
don't
like
people
who are too noisy,
who talk all the time,
who tell lies,
who laugh about my freckles.
I
like
people
who are friendly,
who can listen
and who are honest.

Reconstruction of model text

1 Tell your students that you want them to study the model text carefully.
2 Give them a minute.
3 Then cover the text up.
4 Elicit the text word by word, starting at the last word and working backwards. Write the text on the board as you go along.

Text creation

1 Ask everyone to write their own text based on the model. The following skeleton text might be helpful:

Skeleton text
I don't like people
who___
who___
who___
I like people
who___
who___
and who___

2 Students stick their texts on the poster they have created. Display the posters on the walls around your classroom.

VARIATION
If you work with adults you may want to use the following model text:

I don't like people
who can't listen
who never read books
who smoke when I'm still eating
and who gossip about others.
I like people
who are energetic
who love children
who fight against stupidity
and who care about the fate of our planet.

CHAPTER 3

Question form

QUESTIONS I LIKE, QUESTIONS I HATE

Lead-in activities

Find the questions

1 Write a few words on the board. They should be related to you personally to make the activity motivating for your students, for example:

17 years
Queen Charlotte Islands
red
Yes, I am.

2 Tell your students that these words are answers to personal questions about you that they are supposed to ask you. To avoid lengthy spans of silence help with the questions by using mime.

3 Whenever they successfully elicit one of the answers on the board from you, tick the word(s) concerned. The actual questions to the answers above are:

How long have you been a teacher?
Where are you going for your next holiday?
What colour is your car?
Are you married?

Note, however, that in order to make this activity motivating for your students it is essential that the words you have written on the board are related to you personally.

Interview your teacher

1 Tell your students to imagine that they are doing a personal interview with you. Tell them you will answer any question they ask. Give them time to think of at least three questions.

2 Ask them to write their questions down.

3 Then tell them the following:

Close your eyes and imagine you are asking me your questions one after another. Imagine what answers I am going to give you. Take your time. When you think you know what I'm going to answer, open your eyes again and note down what you think my answers would be.

3.1

GRAMMAR
Questions

LEVEL
Lower
intermediate +

TIME
60 – 80 minutes

EXTRAS
None

4 Put your students into pairs or groups. Tell them to share their questions and the expected answers.

5 Ask your class to sit in a semi-circle with you at the front. Tell them that you are now really going to answer their questions as openly as you can. Say that, although highly unlikely, it could happen that you feel you do not want to answer one of their questions. And if so, you will say the question is too personal.

6 After your students have finished their interviews ask them to compare the answers you gave with the ones they expected. This can be done as a class activity or in small groups. It can trigger off both intensive discussion in class as well as giving you a very good insight into how your students perceive you.

VARIATION
Immediately after you have responded to the question, ask your students to compare each answer with the answer they expected.

Presentation of model text

1 Write the following gapped text on the board:

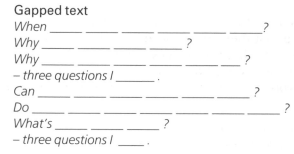

Gapped text
When _____ _____ _____ _____ _____ _____?
Why _____ _____ _____ _____ ?
Why _____ _____ _____ _____ _____ ___ ?
– three questions I _____ .
Can _____ _____ _____ _____ _____ _____ ?
Do _____ _____ _____ _____ _____ _____ _____ ?
What's _____ _____ _____ ?
– three questions I _____ .

2 Ask the class to guess the missing words. Whenever somebody comes up with a correct guess, write it in. We have seen teachers use mime, gesture, nodding, and silent mouthing of words to elicit whole texts from their students without themselves saying a single word. A more direct form of prompting is to give the first letter of a word and get your learners to guess.

   This is the text you should end up with on the board:

Model text
When are you going to do this?
Why didn't you come earlier?
Why didn't you think before you spoke?
– three questions I hate.

Can I talk to you about this?
Do you think what I did is okay?
What's your favourite song?
– three questions I like.

Speculation about the model text

1 Organise your students into pairs. Get them to imagine as many details as they can about the person who wrote the text above. Give them a few questions to guide them, for example:

How old do you think the person is?
What does he/she look like?
What are his/her interests?
Do you think this person would be
interesting to talk to? Give your reasons.
The person mentions six questions in the
text. Who do you think asked these
questions?
Have all the questions been asked by the same person?
Select one of the questions mentioned in
the text. Describe what you think actually happened.

2 Ask each pair to report their findings.

Reconstruction of model text

1 Ask your students to look at the model on the board for a short period of time.
2 Then, while they are still studying the text, quickly rub most of it out leaving only the following:

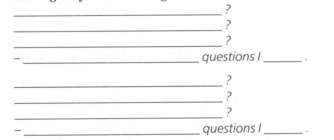

3 After twenty seconds ask students to reconstruct the text orally.

Text creation

Then get them to write a text based on the model. Tell them that they can include any number of questions they want.

Text sharing

Tell your students to stand up, mill around and find a partner. The students read their texts to each other. A lively talk among the pairs might follow. When a pair have finished, they each find another partner to read their texts to.

VARIATION

If you work with adults you may want to use the following model text:

Why didn't you tell me beforehand?
What's the point of all that?
How come you haven't finished?
– three questions I hate.
How was your day?
Would you like to join us?
What other choices have we got?
– three questions I like.

3.2

GRAMMAR
What is +
adjective/noun?

LEVEL
Elementary –
lower
intermediate

TIME
30 – 40 minutes

EXTRAS
None

WHAT'S HARD?

Presentation of model text

Read out the model text.

Model text
What's hard? Tests on Monday.
What's short? Games on Sunday.
What's frightening? An angry teacher.
What's fun? Ice cream after school.

Gathering associations
1 Go to the board and write down the word *school*.
2 Ask your learners to shout words to you. Add all these words onto the board.
3 Form pairs and ask each to group the words from the board under the following headings: *frightening, interesting, difficult, okay, hard, long, relaxing, unfair, great, fun, short.*
4 When they have finished, ask each pair to add words from other topic areas (not school) under each of the headings.
5 Ask each pair to read their words out.

Text creation

1 Ask everyone to lay out their word lists in the centre of the class-room. The spread of papers becomes a word source for writing at step 3.
2 Read out the model text once or twice more.
3 The students write their own texts based on the model. Encourage them to stroll around the centre of the room checking the word lists from time to time.

VARIATION
If you work with adults you may want to use the following model text:

What's hard?
Getting up on Monday mornings.
What's fun?
Watching men ironing.
What's great?
A glass of wine after a hard day's work.
What's relaxing?
Lying in a hot bath.
What's off-putting?
Someone picking their nose.

RAINDROPS ON THE WINDOW

Lead-in activities

The teacher's likes and dislikes
1 Ask your students to write down three things that they think you like and three they think you do not like. Tell them that they should not include anything that everybody knows about you, but speculate about things that are not commonly known about you.
2 After a minute ask everyone to pair up and pool their notes.
3 Pairs join up into groups of four and produce joint lists.
4 One member of each group reads out their speculations to the class. You record the guesses on the board in two columns.
5 Comment on the guesses and ask questions, for example:

Why do you think I don't like pop music? It's true that I like cooking. Do any of you like it too?

The learners' likes and dislikes
1 Get the class into a circle.
2 Toss your ball to someone and address them like this:

Suzanne, do you like animal films?

If Suzanne answers with *yes*, go on asking until her answer is *no*.
3 Then it is her turn to throw the ball to another member of the group. Continue in this way for about three minutes.

Presentation of model text

1 Tell the class that you are going to present a text to them (on OHP) and read it out to them. Tell them they'll have ten seconds to study

3.3

GRAMMAR
Questions with *do*

LEVEL
Elementary

TIME
40 minutes

EXTRAS
A soft ball or a knotted scarf; model text on OHP transparency or poster paper

the text after you finish reading it. Say you'll remove the text and
they'll have to write down what they can remember.

2 Read out the text below.

Reconstruction of model text

1 In pairs, students try to rewrite the whole text.
2 When they have finished, ask someone to come to the board. The
class dictate and this student writes the text on the board.
3 Display the original model text for comparison.

She asked,
'Do you like sport?'
I said no.
She asked,
'Do you read a lot?'
I said no.
She asked,
'Do you like rock music?'
I said no.
She asked,
'What do you like?'
I said,
'Raindrops on the window.'

Text creation

1 Everyone writes two lists about themselves under these headings:

Things lots of people know I don't like
Things not many people know I don't like

2 Students write their own texts based on the model and the prompts
below. Allow about five minutes.

He / she asked,

_____

_____
He / she asked,

_____

_____
He / she asked,

_____

_____
He / she asked,

_____

_____
I said,

_____

3 Presentation of texts.

WHY DOES POPCORN ALWAYS SMELL OF HAMSTERS?

3.4

GRAMMAR
Questions in the third person singular, adverbs of frequency, *taste/smell of, feel/look/sound like*

LEVEL
Lower intermediate

TIME
30 minutes

EXTRAS
One large sheet of poster paper for each group of four to five students; (optional) dictionaries

Lead-in activities

Noun search
1 Ask your learners to work in groups of four.
2 Hand out one large sheet of poster paper to each group.
3 Ask everyone to note down on their sheets of paper as many nouns as they can think of. Countable nouns should be put in the plural, however. Give some examples. If they use dictionaries, encourage them to go beyond what they have been taught so far.

Sentence creation
1 Working in pairs, students create sentences based on the following structure:

Why	does do	. . .	always often sometimes rarely never	taste of smell of sound like look like feel like	. . .

Ask your students to create as many combinations as possible and to include unusual ones such as *Why does popcorn always smell of hamsters?*
2 Elicit their sentences and write them onto a sheet of poster paper.
3 Display the poster on the wall so that everybody can see it easily.

Text creation

1 Ask your class to form new pairs or groups.
2 Ask each group to create a text by selecting some of the sentences from the poster paper and arranging them so that they read like a poem. They may want to give their text a title. Here is an example written in one of the classes in which this technique was tried out:

Why does popcorn always smell of hamsters?
Why does work often taste of tea bags?
Why does poetry sometimes sound like rain?
Why does the lunch break rarely look like roses?
And why does war never sound like music?

3 The students then read out their texts in class.

ACKNOWLEDGEMENT
This lesson has been adapted from an idea in *The Inward Ear* (Maley and Duff 1989, p.138).

3.5

GRAMMAR
Which as
interrogative
pronoun

LEVEL
Intermediate +
(adults)

TIME
40 minutes

EXTRAS
Class set of
gapped text B;
OHP and
transparency

SUCCESS OR FAILURE: WHICH IS MORE DESTRUCTIVE?

Preparation

Write the following words on an OHP transparency:

is lacking	*belong*	*depend on*	*integrity*
realise	*valuable*	*fulfilment*	*fame*
rejoice	*destructive*	*failure*	

Lead-in activity

Remember the words
1 Tell your students that they will have only a few moments to look at the words. They will have to remember them and are not allowed to write anything down.
2 Switch off the OHP. Ask your students to write down as many words as they remember.
3 They then call out the words. You write them on the board.
4 Add the ones they may not have remembered. Ask them to form meaningful sentences with the words.

Presentation of model text A

1 Read out model text A to your class.
2 Ask students to close their eyes. Read the text again, slowly.
3 Say that you are going to read out the text a third time. Ask everyone to note down – while you are reading – any associations they have with the text (e.g. what they disagree with, people or situations they are reminded of, etc.). If necessary, give an example.
4 Then discuss the content of the text. Ask also what associations they had.

Model text A
Fame or integrity: which is more important?
Money or happiness: which is more valuable?
Success or failure: which is more destructive?
If you look to others for fulfilment, you will never truly be fulfilled.
If your happiness depends on money, you will never be happy with yourself.
Be content with what you have;
rejoice in the way things are.
When you realise there is nothing lacking,
the whole world belongs to you.
Lao Tse, *Tao Te Ching* (chapter 44)

In one of the trial classes the students seemed to agree with everything the text says. The teacher got a discussion going by giving a few personal examples:

The text says 'Be content with what you have'. This makes me think of a situation in my life when I really wanted to have a new car. I really wanted to have it. So I finally bought it. Once I had it, it was not at all important for me any more.

Presentation of model text B

1 Hand out copies of gapped text B.
2 Tell your students that each dash stands for a letter. Ask them to fill in the blanks individually and then check with their partner(s).

Gapped text B

Wo _ _ _ o _ act _ _ _ _ : wh _ _ _ a _ _ mo _ _
effe _ _ _ _ _ ?
Lo _ _ _ o_ char _ _ _ _ : wh _ _ _ i_ mo _ _
convi _ _ _ _ _ ?
Know _ _ _ _ _ o_ curi _ _ _ _ _ : wh _ _ _ i_ mo _ _
valu _ _ _ _ ?
It ' _ n _ _ wo _ _ _ th _ _ co _ _ _ ,
it' _ act _ _ _ _ ,
it' _ n _ _ lo _ _ _ th _ _ co _ _ _ ,
it' _ char _ _ _ _ ,
it' _ n _ _ know _ _ _ _ _ th _ _ cou _ _ _ ,
it' _ curi_ _ _ _ _ .

© Longman Group UK Ltd 1992

3 Read out the model text for the final check:

Model text B

Words or actions: which are more
effective?
Looks or charisma: which is more
convincing?
Knowledge or curiosity: which is more
valuable?
It's not words that count,
it's actions,
it's not looks that count,
it's charisma,
it's not knowledge that counts,
it's curiosity.

Text creation

Ask your students to work in pairs and to write their own texts. They can then read them out or display them in the classroom.

NOTE

You might want to tell your students that the *Tao Te Ching* by Lao Tse is an ancient Chinese book of wisdom. Stephen Mitchell's inspiring translation (1988) also contains an excellent introduction.

3.6

GRAMMAR
Who does it belong to?

LEVEL
Lower intermediate +

TIME
30 – 40 minutes

EXTRAS
Cassette of soft, meditative music; several sheets of poster paper, felt-tip pens; class set of model text

THE SMILE ON YOUR FACE

Lead-in activities

Visualisation

1 Play some soft, meditative music. Ask your students to seat themselves comfortably with their backs straight and their bodies in a relaxed position.
2 Lead them into a guided visualisation. For example:

Feel your contact with your chair and the floor . . . allow yourself to relax while you are listening to my voice and the sound of the music . . . and if you want to . . . you can come with me now . . . and imagine that you are now standing in the middle of a beautiful meadow . . . feeling the warmth of the sun on your skin . . . and the gentle breeze . . . and when you look down you can see the soft, green grass and the flowers . . . and you start to walk, feeling the grass under your feet . . . take your time and do everything at your own pace . . . and while you are walking along . . . looking around you . . . seeing all the beautiful colours of the flowers around you . . . and the butterflies and the birds . . . you can feel a sense of freshness and joy . . . take all the time you need to feel the grass and to look around as you walk and then, slowly, at your own pace you return to our classroom . . . take your time . . . slowly open your eyes . . . take a deep breath and stretch a little, welcome back.

Creation of posters

1 Switch off the cassette recorder. Put several sheets of poster paper and a box of felt-tip pens of different colours on the floor.
2 Ask your students to jot down whatever comes to mind (words, sentences, pictures). Play some soft music again while they are doing this.

Reflection
1 Stick all the posters on the wall.
2 Get your students to sit in front of the posters in a semi-circle.
3 Let students comment on the posters, ask each other questions or talk about their experiences during the guided visualisation.

Presentation of model text

1 Give each student a photocopy of the model text below (or show it on the OHP, write it on the board or read it out).

Model text
Who does it belong to,
the blue of the sky
on a beautiful morning in September?
Who does it belong to,
the singing of the birds
in the trees by the river?
Who does it belong to,
the smile on your face
when we happen to meet among the crowd?

© Longman Group UK Ltd 1992

2 Ask your students to study the text for two minutes.
3 Get them to remember the text without looking at it.
4 Elicit the text and write it on the board.

Text creation

1 Clear the text off the board.
2 Ask students to work in pairs and write their own texts following the pattern below, which you can dictate or write on the board.
3 Ask them to think of a title for their text.

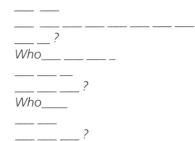

Who does it (do they) belong to,

___ ___

___ ___ ___ ___ ___ ___ ___

___ __ ?

*Who*___ ___ ___ _

___ ___ ___

___ ___ ___ ?

*Who*___

___ ___

___ ___ ___ ?

CHAPTER 4

Complex sentences

MART'S ADVICE

4.1

GRAMMAR
If + present progressive (first conditional), imperatives

LEVEL
Intermediate +

TIME
50 minutes

EXTRAS
OHP transparency of poem 'Mart's advice'; (optional) class set of jumbled text B and gapped text C

Presentation of model text A

1 Display text A on the OHP. Explain any words that you think your students won't be able to guess.
2 Read the poem out twice. The students work in groups of three.
3 Turn off the OHP. Two members of each group try to reconstruct the text in writing from memory. Call up the third member of each group. Show them the text and give them two minutes to study it before returning to their groups.
4 The third student then assists the other two members in reconstructing the text.

Model text A
Mart's advice:

If someone's acting big with you,
if someone's bossing you about,
look very hard at one of their ears.
Keep your eyes fixed on it.
Don't let up.
Stare at it as if it was
a mouldy apple.
Keep staring.
Don't blink.
After a bit
you'll see their hand
go creeping up to touch it.
They're saying to themselves
'What's wrong with my ear?'

At that moment
you know you've won.

Smile.

McGough and Rosen, *You Tell Me*, Puffin Books 1981, p. 31

Checking the text
1 Several groups read out what they have written.
2 Read out the original version again.

3 Present text A on OHP or poster paper aga̶i̶ ̶.̶.̶.̶ so that the students can correct their texts.

Presentation of model text B

1 Hand out a copy of jumbled text B or write it on the board and ask the students to unscramble it.
2 They read their versions out. Then you read out the original.

Jumbled text B
take out a mirror,
'What's this all about?'
or 'Einstein,' 'Karl Marx' or
'the Marx Brothers.'
if someone's laughing at you,
Keep holding it.
Smile, pocket your mirror and then
put your hand in your pocket,
If someone's teasing you,
After a while they'll ask
hold it to their face.
so that you feel very small,
slowly say, 'Freud'
if someone's pulling your leg,

Model text B
If someone's teasing you,
if someone's pulling your leg,
if someone's laughing at you,
so that you feel very small,
put your hand in your pocket,
take out a mirror,
hold it to their face.
Keep holding it.
After a while they'll ask
'What's this all about?'
Smile, pocket your mirror and then
slowly say, 'Freud'
or 'Einstein,' 'Karl Marx' or
'the Marx Brothers.'

© Longman Group UK Ltd 1992

Text creation

1 Ask everyone to write down at least two sentences starting with *I don't like people who* . . . . Ask some students to read out their sentences. For example:
I don't like people who never listen.
I don't like people who complain all
the time.

2 Write a sentence called out by a student on the board.
3 Show your class how to transform this sentence so that it fits the structure of the model text. For example:

I don't like people who never listen
becomes
If somebody never listens to you

I don't like people who never look at me
when I say something
becomes
If someone never looks at me when I say
something

4 Get your learners to transform ten to fifteen sentences in this way.

If somebody always interrupts you
If somebody never cares for your feelings
If somebody never shows any gratitude
If somebody tells you lies
If somebody talks about you behind your back

5 The students write their own texts individually or in pairs. Ask some of them to read their texts to the class or to each other in groups.

The following text was written by a student from a group of advanced adult learners:

If someone is telling stories about you,
if someone is asking you too many questions,
if someone thinks they know everything
better than you,
wait for the moment
when they start babbling.
Take a bucket
hold it in front of their face
and empty it
when they've stopped talking.

4.2

GRAMMAR
Whenever

LEVEL
Lower
intermediate +

TIME
30 minutes

EXTRAS
None

WHENEVER

Presentation of model text

1 Write *whenever* on the board.
2 Tell the students that it is the beginning of a sentence you have in mind. Ask them to shout words to you. Help them to guess what follows by using mime and gesture. Whenever a student gives you a correct word, note it onto the board as below.

Model text
Whenever
my teacher
looks at
me
through
his
thick
glasses
I
feel
very small.

VARIATION

If a student offers a word you aren't looking for, write it to one side and try to use it to build up a new vertical text which incorporates it. Sometimes you can end up with several texts as in figure 9 below. This array was created in one of our trial classes with thirteen-year-olds at the beginning of their third year.

Whenever
my teacher | *I*
gives us | *looks at* | *have*
homework | *me* | *a test* | *a cup*
I'd like | *through* | *I* | *of cocoa*
to say | *his* | | *the world*
'No', | *thick* | *wish* | *seems*
but | *glasses* | *I* | *alright.*
I | *I* | |
don't. | *feel* | *had* | *was*
 | *very* | *the brains* | *a teacher*
 | *small.* | *of* | *not*
 | | *a* | *a pupil.*
 | | *computer.* |

Fig. 9

Text interpretation

1 Get your students to read through the model text again.
2 Ask them to say why the writer feels small. Note their suggestions on the board. This is what a class of thirteen-year-olds came up with:

The writer
– never does his homework
– is new at school
– plays truant
– steals
– doesn't like the teacher
– is always nervous
– is bad at school
– cheats a lot
– plays lots of tricks on his teacher

3 Ask them to speculate what they think the reasons for the person's behaviour could be. Note these speculations on the board too. Here are the suggestions from the above class:

The writer
– comes from a broken home
– has lots of problems with his parents
– is often hit by his parents
– 's mother is dead. His father has no time.
– is stupid
– takes drugs
– watches too much TV
– is a bit crazy

Text creation

Ask your students to create their own texts based on the model text. The following texts were written by learners from the trial class:

Whenever
my dog
eats his
food with
his big
teeth,
I feel
good
because
he doesn't
need any
food for
the rest of
the day.

Whenever
my football team
has lost
a match
our trainer
feels angry,
and
so
do
I.

VARIATION
If you work with adults you may want to use the following model text:

Whenever
my colleagues at work
say a cheerful 'Good morning,'
I ask myself
how those people always manage
to get out of bed
on the right side.

ACKNOWLEDGEMENT
Our thanks to Hans-Eberhard Piepho for the model text (W*henever my teacher . . .*).

IF SHE HAD LOOKED AT ME

Lead-in activities

Questions that change the story
1 Write the following on the board:

| What would have happened if | ... | hadn't ... | (kissed Sleeping Beauty?) |
| | | had ... | (kissed the queen instead of Sleeping Beauty?) |

Announce that you are going to tell a fairy tale, a folk tale or a story. Ask your class to interrupt you whenever they want to.
2 Tell your story, pausing frequently to encourage students to interject past conditional questions. If students do not interrupt you, prompt them somehow (e.g. by gesture). As students ask questions, answer them and adapt the story accordingly. For example:

Student: *What would have happened if Little Red Riding Hood had looked through the window before entering her gran's house?*
Teacher: *She would have known that it wasn't her gran lying in bed. So she would have run back the way she had come, clutching her basket.*
Student: *What would have happened if the wolf had realised that she was running away?*
Teacher: *He would have stormed out of the house to try to catch Little Red Riding Hood. So let's say he was running after the little girl who, however, after a while, happened to look back. When she saw the wolf, she froze ...*

Tell your own story
1 Form groups of four. Each group member should tell a story. The other three in the group must each ask two questions with which they can change the course of the story.
2 Each student finds a partner from another group and tells both their own original story and the story that resulted due to the questions asked in the group phase.

Presentation of model text

1 Hand out the following worksheet (or write both texts as well as the words in the box on the board).
2 Ask everyone to complete the sentences by filling in the gaps with words from the box underneath.

4.3

GRAMMAR
If-sentences + past perfect (third conditional), statements and *wh*-questions

LEVEL
Intermediate +

TIME
50 minutes

EXTRAS
(Optional) Class set of worksheet

WORKSHEET

If she had _____ me
I would have _____ .
If she had _____ at me
I would have _____
_____ for her.
If she had _____ me to
I would have _____ a song.
If she had _____
I would have _____ a poem
and if she had _____ me
I would have said 'Yes.'

If I had _____ her roses
she would have _____ me
and if she had _____ me
I would have _____ her cheek
and if I had _____ her cheek
she would have _____
and if she had _____
I would have _____ her
that her cheeks were
the colour of roses.

kissed – blushed – embraced
– looked at – told – bought –
blushed – asked – written
– embraced – smiled – kissed –
nodded – painted a picture
– blushed – composed – wanted –

3 Ask your students to read out their texts.
4 Present the model texts.

Model texts

If she had looked at me
I would have blushed.
If she had nodded at me
I would have painted
a picture for her.
If she had wanted me to
I would have composed a song.
If she had smiled
I would have written a poem
and if she had asked me
I would have said 'Yes.'

If I had bought her roses
she would have embraced me
and if she had embraced me
I would have kissed her cheek
and if I had kissed her cheek
she would have blushed
and if she had blushed
I would have told her
that her cheeks were
the colour of roses.

Text creation

The students write their own texts based on the model. Follow up with presentations of these texts to the whole class.

I SAID I DIDN'T CARE

Lead-in activities

Quotation from a young adult novel
Read out the following text to your students.

Jeff, a high school student, visits Ellen, a classmate, to apologise for his rude behaviour towards her at school.
'Hey, Ellen,' I said, '. . . listen Ellen, don't cry. Listen . . . I . . . I'm sorry. I didn't mean what I said.'
'Yes, you did,' she said. 'You did mean it.'
'No, I didn't,' I lied. 'It was just a lousy day for me. You know how it is sometimes. You have a lousy day, and you just say stupid things that you don't mean. Honestly, Ellen, I didn't mean it.'

Marilyn Sachs, *The Fat Girl*, Corgi Freeway 1987, p. 45

Personalising the topic
1 Talk about a situation in which you said something different from what you thought or felt.
2 Ask your students what the reason for your behaviour might have been and note their ideas on the board. For example:

fear / not caring / not wanting to hurt / shyness / etc.

Presentation of model text

1 Ask your students to work in pairs at constructing a text from the skeleton below. Allow about five minutes.

Skeleton text A
I s___ I d___'_ c___ ,
b__ I d___'_ f____ g____ i___ t___ ,
I s___ t__ c_____ w__ a g___ i___ ,
b__ I w___'_ s___ w_____ I r_____ f___ I___
g____ ,
a__ I_____ I s___ t___ a d____ w__ f___ w___ m_ ,
b__ I w__ t____ a__ w___ o__
a__ I h____ m_____ f__ d____ t_____
I r_____ d___'_ w___ t_.

© Longman Group UK Ltd 1992

2 Re-form the class. Elicit the completions and add them onto the board.

Model text A
I said I didn't care,
but I didn't fancy going into town,
I said the cinema was a good idea,

4.4

GRAMMAR
Reported speech

LEVEL
Intermediate +

TIME
50 minutes

EXTRAS
(Optional) class sets of skeleton text A and jumbled text B

but I wasn't sure whether I really felt like going,
and later I said that a drink was fine with me,
but I was tired and worn out
and I hated myself for doing things
I really didn't want to.

Interaction
1 Ask your students to write down key words for a situation in which what they said was different from what they thought.
2 Ask them to share their recollections in groups of four.

Second reconstruction

1 Hand out copies of the jumbled text below.
2 Working individually, students put it in the correct order.

VARIATION
Put the text on an OHP or on the board for students to copy.

Jumbled text B
when she explained all the details,
when she showed me her new machine,
But I felt good about my lies
but I thought that
I said 'how interesting'
playing chess with a machine was awful.
because she is such a lovely girl.
but I thought that a computer was
I said 'wow'
I said 'marvellous'
when she played a game on the screen,
but I thought that the view from her room was nice.
the last thing I would buy for myself.   © Longman Group UK Ltd 1992

Model text B
I said 'how interesting'
when she showed me her new machine,
but I thought that a computer was
the last thing I would buy for myself.
I said 'marvellous'
when she explained all the details,
but I thought that the view from her room was nice.
I said 'wow'
when she played a game on the screen,
but I thought that
playing chess with a machine was awful.
But I felt good about my lies
because she is such a lovely girl.

Text creation

1 Following the model, your students write their own texts. Allow about fifteen minutes.
2 Students read their texts out loud.

IF SHE WAS A COLOUR, SHE'D BE PINK

Lead-in activities

Introducing a person
1 Describe the appearance and personality of someone you know well.
2 Read out a text along the lines of the model below to fit the person you have just described.

Model text
A person I like

If he was a colour he'd be beige,
if he was a sound he'd be a low hum,
if he was a smell he'd be rain on a sunny day,
if he was an animal he'd be a bear
and if he was food he'd be a juicy steak.

Collecting words
1 Write a grid on the board and ask everyone to note at least five words for each heading on a sheet of paper.

COLOURS	SOUNDS	SMELLS	ANIMALS	FOOD

Encourage use of bilingual dictionaries. Allow about three or four minutes.
2 Elicit the students' words and write them on the board.

Presentation of model text

1 Hand out copies of the jumbled text overleaf.
2 Ask your students to put the right endings with the right beginnings.
3 Read out the correct version.

4.5

GRAMMAR
If-clause for unreal non-past situations

LEVEL
Intermediate +

TIME
40 minutes

EXTRAS
Class set of jumbled text; a few bilingual dictionaries

Jumbled text
A person I don't like

If he was a colour he'd be a spider,
if he was a sound he'd be porridge,
if he was a smell he'd be a dirty grey,
if he was an animal he'd be burning tyres,
and if he was food he'd be the hissing of a snake. © Longman Group UK Ltd 1992

Model text
A person I don't like

If he was a colour he'd be a dirty grey,
if he was a sound he'd be the hissing of a snake,
if he was a smell he'd be burning tyres,
if he was an animal he'd be a spider,
and if he was food he'd be porridge.

Text creation

Ask your students to write their own texts. They can write about a good friend, someone in their family, people they know from the media, etc. Tell them not to forget to give their text a title.
The following text was written by a fourteen-year-old student:

A person I don't like

If he was a colour he'd be a dirty yellow,
if he was a sound he'd be the grunting of a pig,
if he was a smell he'd be petrol,
if he was an animal he'd be an elephant,
and if he was food he'd be a fat chicken.

4.6

GRAMMAR
Reported
commands

LEVEL
Lower
intermediate +

TIME
40 minutes

EXTRAS
Class set of text A

I TOLD YOU NOT TO CLOSE IT

Lead-in activities

Mime the action
1 Ask your students to work in groups of four. They decide on four actions to mime, e.g. *eating spaghetti*, *riding a bike*, *playing table tennis*, etc. Allow about three minutes.
2 Re-form your class. Ask one student from each group to come to the front of the class. One after the other, ask them to start miming. The other students try to guess, for example:

Are you playing the guitar?
Are you making pizza?

Presentation of model texts

1 Hand out copies of model text A and ask your students to read it to themselves.

Model text A

I told him not to open the door with a hammer,
I told him not to sit on the vase,
I told him not to try to catch the
birds in the cherry tree,
I told him not to eat the cactus,
I told him not to feed the cat with the goldfish.
Phew! Isn't he a bloody nuisance.

© Longman Group UK Ltd 1992

2 Say you are going to read a similar but different text twice. Tell your students not to write anything down until you have finished reading it out. Their task is to change text A according to what they hear (text B).
3 Read model text B twice.
4 Students read out their new version. Comment on accuracy.
5 Read text B out again. Students compare their texts with text B and correct.

Model text B

I told him not to open the can with a spoon,
I told him not to eat the flowers in the vase,
I told him not to jump down from the balcony,
I told him not to drink the perfume,
I told him not to cut the cat's claws.
Phew! Isn't he a bloody nuisance.

Making lists

1 Students work in groups of four to write ten sentences of the pattern:

I / She / He told him / her / me not to . . . (paint the kitchen with honey)

If there are five groups, each group makes five copies of their list of sentences, if there are six groups, each writes six copies and so on.
2 Each group hands one copy to each of the other groups and keeps one for themselves.

Text creation

1 Choosing from the raw material contained in their various lists, each group writes a text structured like text B. But encourage them to think of their own ending.
2 They then read their texts out loud.

This text was written by a fourteen-year-old in his fourth year of English.

I told her not to put jam into her
enemy's hair,
I told her not to water the flowers
with our best wine,
I told her not to lock her little
brother into the lion's cage,
I told her not to put poisonous snakes
into her parents' bedroom,
I told her not to burn down the school,
but she didn't listen and now
she writes postcards from a place
right in the centre of the Sahara.

VARIATION

If you work with adults you may want to use the following model text:

I told him not to try
to repair the washing machine,
I told him not to forget
to keep the dog on the lead,
I told him not to water
the cacti every day,
I told him not to mow
the lawn at midnight.
And do you know what he said?
'Didn't I do nicely?'

CHILDHOOD DREAMS

Preparation

Make enough copies of text A for each group of four students. Cut each copy into one line strips. Copy a photo like the one in figure 10 for each pair of students.

Lead-in activity

Picture associations
1 Ask your students to work in pairs. Hand out a photocopy of a photograph similar to the one below to each pair.
2 Ask the students to jot down, on one sheet of paper, as many words as they can that they associate with the picture.

Fig. 10

Structuring word fields
1 Ask the pairs to shout their words to you. Write them on the board.
2 Rub out the words. Then, getting students to help you recall what was on the board, rewrite the words in some kind of principled arrangement. For example, parts of speech in columns of different colours or in mind map form (see figure 11 overleaf). Leave this on the board as a help for the students in the writing phase.

Thinking back
1 Tell your learners about a childhood dream you had.
2 Give each student a copy of the list overleaf. Ask everyone to write down key words for dreams they had at the times of their lives mentioned in the list. Depending on the age of your learners, you might have to adapt the grid.

4.7

GRAMMAR
Second conditional

LEVEL
Lower intermediate +

TIME
40 minutes

EXTRAS
Class set of time-phrases list and photo

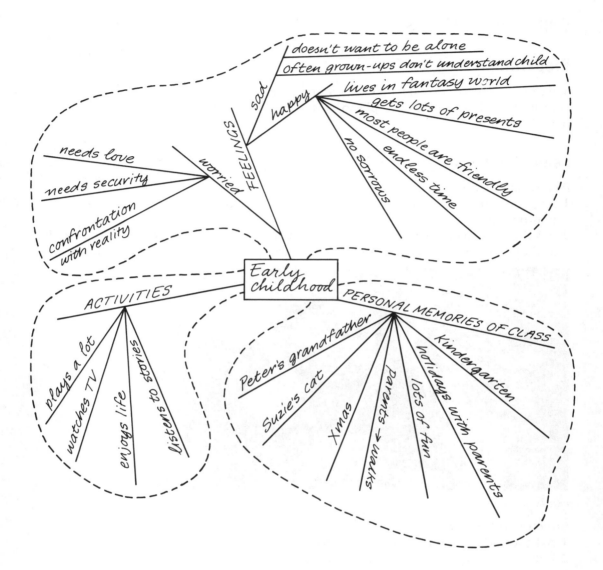

Fig. 11

Dream
Last year
Three years ago
Five years ago
Ten years ago
Fifteen years ago
Twenty years ago

Group reflection

Ask your students to talk about their dreams in groups. In a class of lower intermediate learners it might be helpful to write the following language on the board:

Last year		*having . . .*
Three years ago		*getting . . .*
Five years ago	*I dreamt of*	*winning . . .*
Ten years ago		*being . . .*
Fifteen years ago		*being able to . . .*
Twenty years ago		*making . . .*

Presentation and reconstruction of model text

1 Keeping the same groups, hand out your strips of the model text.
2 Ask them to put the strips in order as you read the text. (Read it twice.)

Model text
With a lot more money
I could buy
a horse and a hot air balloon.
With a lot more time
I could build myself a tree house
in the old oak.
What a pity
that I don't have
more spare time
and a lot of money.
Or am I just lucky
to have what I have?

Text creation

Ask your learners to write their own texts following the model text. If you think it necessary, write the following skeleton on the board:

Skeleton text
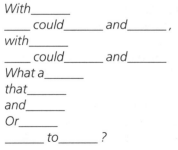
With_____
____ could_____ and_____ ,
with_____
____ could_____ and_____
What a_____
that_____
and_____
Or_____
_____ to_____ ?

Text sharing

Collect the finished texts and mount them, possibly along with some photos, on poster paper for display on the wall. The students stroll about and read the texts.

ACKNOWLEDGEMENT
The technique of mind mapping comes from Tony Buzan. See Buzan 1974 for more on this form of representation.

4.8

GRAMMAR
I wish I + past

LEVEL
Lower
intermediate +

TIME
45 minutes

EXTRAS
Class set of
worksheets;
substitution
table on OHP
transparency or
big sheet of
poster paper

I WISH I HAD ...

Lead-in activities

What's on his/her mind
1 Draw the picture in figure 12 on the board. Draw a thought bubble above the person's head and write into it: *I wish I had . . .*
2 Ask your students for various completions of the sentence.

Fig. 12

Wishes I have
Present the following on poster or OHP and ask the class to say sentences out loud:

I wish	I had I was / were I lived I could I wasn't / weren't I didn't	in another country / play the piano / stronger / tidier / so careless / so tired / solve my problems / more time / in another country / alone / with my girl (woman, guy, man) / a flat of my own / a new bike / a new television / help him(her) / live in . . . / remember it / understood it / a good friend / in love / ill / understand it / live in peace / a coward / have to do it / have to leave /

For example:

Student: *I wish I lived in another country.*
Teacher: *Where would you like to live?*
Student: *In . . .*

React to the sentences in a natural way.

Try to remember
1 Tell your class to study the substitution table on the previous page for a minute without writing anything down.
2 Cover it up and ask everyone to write down as many sentences as they can remember.
3 Invite individual students to read out their sentences. When half of the class have read their sentences, ask the remaining students each to choose one particularly meaningful sentence from their own list. Ask them to say that sentence out loud.

Presentation of model texts

1 Form groups of three.
2 Hand out a copy of the worksheet below to each student. The students work together to try to fill in the missing words.

WORKSHEET

Text A *I wish I had more _____ .*
       I wish I wasn't _____ .

       I wish my fingers _____ quiet
       and I wish I wasn't thinking of
       _____ my hands
       round the neck of the fat man
       who had just _____ the queue.

blow up / noise / jumped /
patience / planning /
nervous / interesting / lose /
punctual / crying /
thumbs / animal /
would keep / listening /
putting / raising /
voice / laughing

Text B *I wish I wasn't so _____ .*
       I wish I had the _____ to talk to her.
       I wish I could hold my _____ up high.
       I wish I wasn't feeling so _____
       like a kitten
       _____ in the rain.

jumped / tired / knee /
happy / nervous /
courage / kept /
raising / head / staring /
crying / small / lost /
putting / laughing

Comparison of texts
1 Some of the students read their versions to the whole class.
2 Read out the versions below. Tell everyone to check their texts against the originals.

Model text A

I wish I had more patience.
I wish I wasn't nervous.
I wish my fingers would keep quiet
and I wish I wasn't thinking of
putting my hands
round the neck of the fat man
who has just jumped the queue.

Model text B

I wish I wasn't so nervous.
I wish I had the courage to talk to her.
I wish I could hold my head up high
and I wish I wasn't feeling so small
like a kitten
lost in the rain.

NOTE

In the texts above *were/weren't* could be used instead of *was/wasn't*.

Text creation

1 Learners write their own texts using those above as models. Make it clear to them that they should follow the same grammatical framework (*I wish . . .*), but add their own ideas and ending.
2 They can then read their texts out loud.

NOTE

In step one of *What's on his/her mind?* we have suggested using stick drawing figures. An excellent book on how to draw them is *1,000 Pictures for Teachers to Copy* (Wright 1984).

4.9

GRAMMAR
Reported speech

LEVEL
Intermediate +

TIME
60 minutes

EXTRAS
Several copies of
the model text

LIES, LIES, LIES

Lead-in activities

Spot the lies
Write some statements about yourself on the board and get your students to decide whether they think they are true or lies. You score a point when the students consider something that is true to be a lie and vice versa. If the group cannot decide, take a majority vote. For example:

Teacher: *My grandmother was born in Ireland.*
When I was a child we kept chickens in our cellar.
I once travelled round Cornwall on a tandem bike.
My favourite series on TV is . . .
I hate spinach and would never eat it.

What's your score?

1 Tell the students to pick a partner they do not know very well.

2 Both write down five sentences which they then read out to their partner, who guesses whether the sentence is true or a lie. The one who guesses scores a point for each correct guess. For example:

Student 1: When I was a child I had a cat as a pet.
Student 2: True.
Student 1: No, it's a lie, I always wanted to have one
but I was never allowed to keep a pet.
(No point for Student 2)

3 Get the class into a circle. Each student reports their score and gives just one example of something they guessed wrong. It might be helpful to write the following on the board.

Hisako/Alain said she/he | *had . . .*
| *had met . . .*
| *had been to . . .*
I thought it was a lie (true), but it's true (a lie).

Presentation of model text

1 Put three to six copies of the model text up on the walls around your room. There should be at least one copy for each three students. Ask your students to copy it onto sheets of paper which they must leave at their desks or tables. That is, since the text is not in large lettering, everyone has to get up, read part of the text, go back to their seat, write down what they remember, go back to the text and read a bit more, and so on.

Model text
He told us he had an uncle in Japan
and he said
they had spent their holidays in
Hawaii
and he added
that his father had bought a Porsche
and he told us that they had a house
as big as the school building
but then we found out
that he was just like us,
but a liar.

© Longman Group UK Ltd 1992

2 When everyone has finished, read out the text. Students check their copies. (Perhaps, as you read, stroll around and check that everyone is producing an accurate copy.)

ACKNOWLEDGEMENT
We learnt this technique from Mario Rinvolucri.

Text creation

Everyone writes their own text based on the model and presents it to the class. The following text was written by a fourteen-year-old student at the beginning of the fourth year of English.

She told us
that her father had the biggest
Mercedes in the world
and that her room was bigger than the
school building
and that she had got a swimming pool
in it.
She added that her mother had been a
famous model fourteen years ago
but then we found out
that all she had told us
was big, fat lies.

Lies don't pay
1 Tell your group about a time you or somebody else told a lie and regretted having done so.
2 Write the key words from the story on the board.
3 Allow a few minutes for the class to think about a time somebody lied. It does not matter whether they experienced the situation themselves or whether they heard/read about it or saw it in a film.
4 Tell them to write about the situation using key words only. Give an example.
5 Ask a student for his or her key words. Write them on the board. Invite the others to flesh out the story individually or in groups.

VARIATION
If you work with adults you may want to use the following model text:

My new acquaintance told me
he loved parachuting
he said he went to the theatre
at least once a week
he added that he had played in an
orchestra some time ago
and he mentioned
that he had travelled all over the
world,
but he forgot to tell me
that all these things
had only happened inside his head.

IF THEY ASKED ME TO CUT MY HAIR

Lead-in activity

Building sentences

1 Write a second conditional sentence on the board, for example:

If she went to the party with that idiot,
I'd eat my hat.

If you think it necessary, explain that the sentence describes an improbable situation and does not refer to past time.

2 Display a list of prompts such as those below and ask everyone to say sentences like, *If someone I liked laughed at me, I'd feel hurt.*

stole my bike	*cut off . . . hair*
bit	*bite back*
helped with the homework	*be glad*
invited . . . to a party	*say 'No'*
asked for money	*give it . . .*
baked a cake	*make spaghetti*
told . . . to shut up	*slam the door*
called . . . an idiot again	*scream*
gave . . . .a bad mark	*be angry*
laughed at . . .	*feel hurt*

3 When all of the ten sentences have been formed, remove the prompts and ask individual students which sentence they liked best. It does not matter if the same sentence is mentioned more than once.
4 Then give your class about five minutes to write down three sentences following the pattern of the examples above.
5 Ask several students to read their sentences out.

Presentation of model text

1 Read out the model text twice. Your students should not write anything down.
2 After the second reading, they try to reconstruct the text individually.
3 In pairs or groups of three, students compare notes. Each group/pair agrees on a full version.
4 They read their texts back to you.
5 If there are discrepancies from the model text, read it again to allow for another check.

GRAMMAR
If-clause
+ past (second conditional)

LEVEL
Intermediate +

TIME
40 – 50 minutes

EXTRAS
None

Model text
If they asked me to cut my hair
I'd grow it long.
If they told me to tidy up my room
I'd make a mess.
If they ordered me to study harder
I'd burn my books.
But the trouble is
that they leave me alone
and I hate them for that.

Text creation

1 Give your students the following skeleton text and ask them to write their own texts. Instead of *I/me* the students may, of course, use *he/him, she/her, we/us, they/them*.

Skeleton text
If they asked me _____
I'd _____
If they told me _____
I'd _____
If they ordered me _____
I'd _____
But the trouble is
that _____
and I _____

© Longman Group UK Ltd 1992

2 Publication of texts.

VARIATION
If you work with adults you may want to use the following model text:

If she asked me
to give up cigarettes,
I'd start smoking cigars.
If she told me
to help with the washing up,
I'd break all the plates.
If she asked me
to do the shopping,
I'd spend the money in a pub.
If she asked me
to stop eating chips
I'd gorge myself on them.
But she accepts me
the way I am
and that drives me mad.

MEMORIES

Preparation

Photocopy the model text: you need one text per group of four learners. Cut the text up line by line. Write words (see p. 129) on slips of paper, one word per slip, written rather small so that the students have to get up if they want to read them.

LESSON ONE

The aim of this activity is to make students aware of sensory areas and their own use of and preferences for certain ones.

Lead-in activities

1 Tell your students that different people frequently call to mind very different kinds of sensory experiences when a word makes an impression on them. Thus a word like *bell* might have a very strong visual impact on a person, who may literally *see* a colour picture of a bell when they 'think' of this word. Whereas another person, might actually *hear* the sound of the church bell of the village in which he used to live years ago. A third person might actually have the *feeling* of touching the metal surface of a bell. And there are people who may have two or more different kinds of such vivid sensory memories at the same time.
2 Give each student a grid (see figure 13).
3 Tell them that you are going to read them a list of words. They should write each word in the column on the left and tick the sensory area(s) that they link the word with.

4.11

GRAMMAR
Gerund

LEVEL
Intermediate +

TIME
2 lessons of 40 minutes each

EXTRAS
Class sets of figure 13, the cut-up model text and a copy of the skeleton text for each pair; 30 slips of adhesive paper (or use Blu-Tack); felt-tip pens; visuals (photos, drawings) for collages

word	visual (seeing)	auditory (hearing)	kinaesthetic (feeling, touching, moving)	gustatory (tasting)	olfactory (smelling)
bell		✓			

Fig. 13

© Longman Group UK Ltd 1992

4 Read out the following words to your class (or any words you want):

> *wind – bunch of flowers – beef steak –*
> *modern painting – mushroom – lake – bike –*
> *mother – father – belt – pop music – cat –*
> *chocolate bar*

5 Ask your students to compare their results in groups. You could write the following guiding questions on the board:

Which word(s) mostly triggered off the same sensory memories in the group? Which word(s) triggered off the most different sensory memories in the group?

From your results, would you say you are the kind of person who experiences most through what you see, what you hear or through what you can touch or feel?

How far do your findings correspond to what you expected?

Stem sentences

Present the following prompts and ask your students to write sentences and read them out later. They might wish to include some of the nouns from the grid above but they should also use other words. For example, *Smelling horses makes me think of Western films.*

Listening to	
Hearing	
Watching	
Seeing . . .	*makes me think of . . .*
Feeling	*brings back memories of . . .*
Touching	
Smelling	
Tasting	

Presentation of model text

1 Form pairs and give each a copy of the skeleton text below.

Skeleton text
Listening to _____
talking about the _____
you wanted to _____ and never _____
makes me _____
of the _____ that I wanted to write
and never _____ .
It also brings back _____ of _____
I wanted to _____ better
and never _____ .
I _____ if I will ever
say the _____ to you
that I'd _____ to say.

© Longman Group UK Ltd 1992

2 Stick slips of paper on the walls of your room. Each slip should bear one of the following words:

get to know	like	song
memories	things	truth
wonder	did	book
think	did	say
you	letters	intended
cross	summer holidays	make
finished	chocolate pudding	tasks
bamboo bridge	have	happy
people	poem	sing

3 Get your students to complete the text by walking around the classroom searching for the words they need. Tell the students that there are more slips than gaps.
4 Ask the pairs to read out loud the texts they have created.

LESSON TWO

Presentation of model text

Read out the text below just once.

Model text
Listening to you
talking about the bamboo bridge
you wanted to cross and never did
makes me think
of the letters that I wanted to write
and never finished.
It also brings back memories of people
I wanted to get to know better
and never did.
I wonder if I will ever
say the things to you
that I'd like to say.

© Longman Group UK Ltd 1992

Reconstruction of model text

1 Arrange your learners in groups.
2 Hand out the cut-up model text to each group.
3 Ask your learners to unjumble the strips.

Text creation

1 Write down the following words on the board.

Listening to . . . (Hearing . . . / Watching . . .)
makes . . . of
It also brings back memories of . . .
I wonder if . . .

2 Ask your learners to write a text based on the model.

Presentation of text

1 Ask your students to create a visual (collage/drawing etc.) which they think fits the text they have created.
2 Display the texts and the visuals in class.

The following two texts were written by colleagues during an in-service training workshop in Paris.

Hearing you humming 'Danny Boy'
makes me think of the time
when I was a very small child.
It also brings back memories of peace
and happiness and beauty.
I wonder
if Northern Ireland
will ever become
peaceful and happy again.
Helen Bouvy

Smelling roses
makes me think of cider
it also brings back
memories of English gardens.
I wonder
if I'll ever have a garden.
Mandy Weyer-Brown

4.12

GRAMMAR
Relative pronouns *who*, *whose*

LEVEL
Intermediate +

TIME
50 minutes

EXTRAS
A cassette of soft, meditative music

I'D LIKE TO GET TO KNOW A WOMAN

Lead-in activities

A person I'd like to get to know
1 Ask your students to write down the name of a person they would like to get to know. Allow two or three minutes.
2 Ask them for the names they have come up with, write them on the board and ask them why they would like to get to know these people.

A daydream
1 Invite your students to accompany you on a short trip. Tell them to sit comfortably with their backs straight. Begin to play some soft meditative music and guide them through a visualisation, for example:

I want you to imagine that you are sitting in an aeroplane ... the plane is taking off and you lean back in your comfy seat ... the plane is going higher and higher and you can see the blue sky ... you relax and lean back and dream ... and after some time you can feel the plane slowly going down and down until you feel it touch the ground and come to a standstill.

When you now get off the plane, you can see this marvellous beach with palm trees right in front of you. There is a small path which you follow down to the beach. You can feel the sand under your feet, the warmth of the sun on your skin and you hear the wind in the palm trees and the waves of the ocean. And there, right on the beach, a person is looking out at the sea, and when this person turns round you see that it is someone you have wanted to get to know for a long time. And you both sit down in the warm sand and begin to talk. Take all the time you need for your talk ...

(allow two minutes)

... Now as the sun goes down, you realise that the time has come for you to say good-bye, and you slowly walk back along the little path to the aeroplane that is waiting for you. And you get on and it slowly takes off and safely takes you back to our classroom here. And while you are slowly coming back you very clearly remember the person you got to know on the beach in that foreign country. Come slowly back now and open your eyes with a feeling of freshness and joy.

2 Ask your students to share what they experienced in pairs. Some might even be willing to share with the whole group.

VARIATION
1 Suggest that everyone writes down key words about their experience during the creative visualisation.
2 Form pairs. Student A tries to guess from the key words who Student B met, what they talked about and so on. B comments on the accuracy of A's guesses. Then B guesses about A.

Presentation and reconstruction of model text

1 Display the model text. Omit all occurrences of *who* and *whose*.
2 Elicit the missing words.
3 Read the text out loud.
4 Cover up or rub out words of your choice (e.g. all the verbs).
5 Elicit a reconstruction of the text. Do this three or four times. Delete different words each time.
6 Leave more and more gaps until no prompts are left and students are repeating the whole text from memory.

Model text
I'd like to get to know
a woman
who has golden eyes
who wears snakes as necklaces
whose pet is a toad
whose friends are sorcerers
and who,
if I want her to,
slips into a bottle
I keep at my bedside.

Text creation

1 Display a skeleton of the model text. Students write their own texts.

Skeleton text
I'd like to get to know
a _____
_____ has _____
_____ wears _____
_____ pet is _____
_____ friends _____
and _____
if I want _____ to

_____

2 Publication of texts.

Here are two texts, the first written by an advanced student, the other by a colleague.

I'd like to get to know
somebody
who has some mountains of his own
who wears a hat made of flowers
whose pet is an eagle
whose friends are the stars and the clouds
and who'll take me with him
for a flight
if I want to be free.
Katrin Zangl

I'd like to get to know
a wise woman
who is another version of myself
who has all the answers
who sees in the dark
whose eyes are knowing
whose smile is mysterious
and who,
if I want her to,
will tell me all her secrets.
Jackie Smith

Bibliography

Asher, J 1986 *Learning Another Language Through Actions: The Complete Language Teacher's Guidebook* Sky Oaks Productions

Ballinger, E et al 1991 *Conrad and Company* Österreichischer Bundesverlag

Bourke, J M 1989 *The Grammar Gap* English Teaching Forum

Buzan, T 1974 *Use Your Head* Ariel Books, BBC

Davis, P and Rinvolucri, M 1988 *Dictation* CUP

Davis, P and Rinvolucri, M 1990 *The Confidence Book* Longman

Dilts, R B , Eppstein, T and Dilts, R W *Tools for Dreamers: Strategies for Creativity and the Structure of Innovation* Meta Publications

Frank, C and Rinvolucri M, 1987 *Grammar in Action* Prentice Hall

Graham, C 1978 *Jazz Chants* OUP

Graham, C 1979 *Jazz Chants for Children* OUP

Grinder, M 1989 *Righting the Educational Conveyor Belt* Metamorphous Press

Hess, N 1991 *Headstarts* Longman

Houston, J 1982 *The Possible Human* J P Tarcher Inc

Klauser, H A 1986 *Writing on Both Sides of the Brain. Breakthrough Techniques for People Who Write* Harper and Row

Kuskin, K 1980 *Dogs and Dragons, Trees and Dreams* Harper and Row

Landers, A 1968 *Truth is Stranger. . .* Prentice Hall

Maley, A and Duff, A 1989 *The Inward Ear* CUP

Mazer, N F 1983 *Someone to Love* Delacorte Press

McGough, R and Rosen, M 1981 *You Tell Me* Puffin Books

Meister Vitale, B 1982 *Unicorns Are Real* Jalmar Press

Mitchell, S 1988 *Tao Te Ching (A New English Version)* Harper and Row

Morgan, J and Rinvolucri, M 1986 *Vocabulary* OUP

Moskowitz, G 1978 *Sharing and Caring in the Foreign Language Classroom* Newbury House

Rinvolucri, M 1984 *Grammar Games* CUP

Rosen, M 1981 *Wouldn't You Like to Know* Puffin Books

Rutherford, W 1987 *Second Language Grammar: Learning and Teaching* Longman

Sachs, M 1987 *The Fat Girl* Corgi Freeway

Stanford, G 1977 *Developing Effective Classroom Groups* Hart Publishing Company

Stevick, E 1976 *Memory, Meaning and Method* Newbury House

Stevick, E 1989 *Success With Foreign Languages* Prentice Hall

Swan, M 1980 *Practical English Usage* OUP

Ur, P 1988 *Grammar Practice Activities* CUP

Woods, E and McLeod, N 1990 *Using English Grammar. Meaning and Form* Prentice Hall

Wright, A 1984 *1,000 Pictures for Teachers to Copy* Collins